the
Cookies & Cups
COOKBOOK

the
Cookies & Cups
COOKBOOK

125+ sweet & savory recipes
reminding you to
Always Eat Dessert First

SHELLY JARONSKY

Gallery Books

NEW YORK   LONDON   TORONTO   SYDNEY   NEW DELHI

G

Gallery Books
An Imprint of Simon & Schuster, Inc.
1230 Avenue of the Americas
New York, NY 10020

First Gallery Books trade paperback edition April 2016

GALLERY BOOKS and colophon are registered trademarks of Simon & Schuster, Inc.

For information about special discounts for bulk purchases, please contact Simon & Schuster Special Sales at 1-866-506-1949 or business@simonandschuster.com.

The Simon & Schuster Speakers Bureau can bring authors to your live event. For more information or to book an event, contact the Simon & Schuster Speakers Bureau at 1-866-248-3049 or visit our website at www.simonspeakers.com.

Interior design by Jaime Putorti
Photography by Shelly Jaronsky

Manufactured in the United States of America

10 9 8 7 6 5 4 3 2 1

Library of Congress Cataloging-in-Publication Data

Jaronsky, Shelly.
The cookies & cups cookbook : 125+ sweet and savory recipes reminding you to always eat dessert first / by Shelly Jaronsky
        pages ; cm
1. Desserts. 2. Cookies. I. Title. II. Title: Cookies and cups cookbook.
TX773.J365   2016
641.86—dc23
                                2015027541
ISBN 978-1-5011-0251-6
ISBN 978-1-5011-0256-1 (ebook)

TO MY BOYS,

Chris, Christopher, David, Jake, and Max,

THE LOVES OF MY LIFE

CONTENTS

❧ Part One: Dessert First ❧

❧ Part Two: Did You Save Room for Dinner? ❧

INTRODUCTION

I'm gonna talk a little about me right now.

*H*i. Hello. Oh hey.

So here we are. You're reading, I'm writing. A book. OMG a book.

Hi. How should we start?

I'm Shelly. Let's be food friends. No, that's weird.

Okay, let's just chat. First off, thanks for reading this part. I am the worst about glancing over all the WORDS in cookbooks and skipping to the pictures. I am guessing I am not the only one. I certainly expect my family and loved ones to read this (Hi, Dad!), but if you are not related to me and are still with me here, I love you forever!

Again.

Hi.

So I wrote a book. A cookbook. With food I want you to make and love and share.

✤ Let's Begin at the End . . . ✤

In the kitchen I live by few rules. I get asked ALL THE TIME, "What do you do with all those desserts?" Well, I try them. ALL. Some I eat entirely too much of, but most of the time I practice a moderate amount of self-control and give the food away. A brownie isn't going to hurt me. A whole tray of brownies might.

But really, dessert has always come first for me. It's my favorite meal. I choose restaurants based on the dessert menus alone. It's the truth. Now I can claim it's all in the name of research, but let's be honest, dessert is fun. Dessert is a treat. Dessert is special.

And why not eat dessert first? Whoever made up the rule that desserts are a leftover thought "if you have room" is my mortal enemy. Nobody puts Baby in the corner.

So my book, like my life and my website, is a little backwards.

A normal cookbook has all your foods: appetizers, soups, entrees . . . with one tiny little chapter, barely a footnote, if you will, reserved for desserts.

I CRY INJUSTICE!

In my world desserts are the headline act. I mean, why not?

So yep, that's what's happening here. Desserts run the show. I've got tons of amazing, brand-new sweet recipes for you, along with a few of your favorites from my website. PLUS a whole section at the end of the book set aside for some epic mealtime savories.

I hope you can trust my crazy for a bit and sit back and enjoy. I want you to dog-ear the crap out of this book. I want it to be the stained, sticky-paged, marked-up book that you come back to time and time again.

I want to be in your kitchen with you, and this is my shot.

❧ Okay, Now the Beginning . . . ❧

My love for baking (and cooking) began when I was a small girl in my grandma's kitchen. I used to spend entire summers with my grandparents. My parents would just ship me off after the school year was over and pick me up at the airport a week before summer break ended.

You think I'm exaggerating? I'm totally not.

But that was just fine by me. I loved it at my grandparents' house. LOVED.

We shopped, we played golf, we swam, we baked, and all the focus was on me. Yes, I am a huge brat with possible narcissistic tendencies because of this, but that's neither here nor there.

My grandparents' house was the best. The pantry was always stocked with Kraft Macaroni & Cheese and Pop-Tarts, my favorite foods then, now, and forevermore. My grandma and I would craft together, host dinner parties together, and paint our nails together, and my grandpa used to make those amazing frosting-filled graham cracker sandwiches (which are still one of my favorite food groups), eat saltines slathered with butter, and head to McDonald's every morning at ten for a biscuit and coffee. He even kept a little tin under his chair at night specifically for his Hershey's Kisses wrappers. A favorite food memory of my grandpa is back in the late '80s when SlimFast first came out. Everyone was doing it. So one summer my grandparents went on that liquid meal plan, only my grandpa would mix his SlimFast with ice cream. Not nonfat milk . . . or water . . . or whatever the blend was supposed to be. ICE CREAM. Seriously. I'm not sure how much weight he actually lost, but I am sure it made the diet way more delicious. My point is, it doesn't take a genius to figure out how I ended up with a blog made up of 80 percent sweets.

It's not my fault, folks. I blame Slim-Fast.

P.S. My grandpa is still alive and kickin' at ninety-three years.

Anyhow, beyond the SlimFast, my first memory of creating a recipe was with my grandma in her kitchen making monkey bread. We would make it at least once a week, changing it up a bit each time and taking it over to a neigh-bor's house for "coffee hour." Now, as a kid I hated coffee hour. All the adults sitting around talking was so boring. BUT the creating of the monkey bread made all the boring adult conversations totally worth it.

During the not-summer months I lived out most of my childhood in Houston, Texas. (I truly believe all people should be lucky enough to live in Texas at one point in their lives.) Then after college I moved to New Jersey. Yes, on purpose.

You see, my one true love called the Garden State home, which meant that Texas had to be left behind. The move was a tough choice, but love won out. I still live in New Jersey and I'm married to the same dude.

We now have a family with four boys and two ridiculous dogs named Polly and Chewie. Happily ever after.

❧ But Wait, There's More . . . ❧

So how did I go from being a displaced Texan to sitting here writing a cookbook? Well, thanks for asking! Before I had kids I had a few jobs that were totally not for me and totally not worth talking about really . . . but then after my last little nugget was born I decided I needed something to do. A J.O.B.

I loved cooking every night for my family, but what I loved most was making desserts. Unfortunately I've heard you, like, shouldn't eat desserts all the time.

Stupid, I know.

So one day in 2008, I was online poking around for a recipe and I came across a food blog. I really had no idea what a food blog was, but it seemed like something I would like to try! It gave me a justification for excessive dessert making. I mean, any job that makes baking a giant chocolate cake on a Tuesday morning acceptable . . . well, I want in.

And just like that, I started my website. Let me share a moment of truth with you on the title of my website: It took me about 2.67 seconds to settle on a name. Branding be DAMNED! The only thought involved was that I knew I loved cookies, duh. And I also loved peanut butter cups and cupcakes and I used measuring cups and, well . . .

So, yep. Cookiesandcups.com. It's certainly not a genius title . . . sometimes people are like, "Cups? Like mugs?" Ugh. No. Anyway, I chose it and I am not a quitter. So six years later here I am, still running a website with a confusing name.

Originally I started my site just sharing pictures of the desserts I was making in hopes that someone out there would see them and want me to bake for them too. Being a cookie decorator seemed like a dream job for me at that time, so I just started taking really horribly lit pictures of cute cookies and cupcakes I baked and posted them on my site along with a few incomplete sentences, hoping the phone would start ringing.

It didn't. Shocking, I know.

Luckily I have some great friends, and with a little word of mouth I was baking regularly for customers. At first it was fun. I really put my heart into it that first year or so. The thing is, occasionally on my website I would share a recipe for something I had made instead of just the picture, and that's when I started getting the real feedback. People were actually baking the recipes I posted! I found tremendous joy in this. More joy, I'd say, than decorating cookies shaped like frogs and shipping them off to Michigan, only to find out that four out of the twelve cookies broke somewhere over Pennsylvania.

So gradually my website started to shift from a showcase of sorts, to a recipe source. And I was loving it. Creating my own recipes was where I found my groove. After one massive Yankee Stadium Cake FAIL I decided to throw in the towel at cake/cookie decorating. Making a cake that looked like a building was decidedly NOT the direction I wanted to continue going in. Playing around with flavors and ingredients was the part that I liked the best. Just like back in my grandma's kitchen making monkey bread, trying a little something different each time, I'd finally found my niche.

The more I posted recipes, the more people were reading and, more important, commenting! Building a relationship over the past eight years with the people who read my site has been such a privilege. My website has allowed me to not only bake and create thousands of recipes but it has also introduced me to people around the world whom I would never have otherwise gotten the chance to know. It's also given me the opportunity to work with some amazing people, to visit places I never would have thought I would get to see, and to use the word "work" in a way that makes my heart go pitter-patter. It's been a blessing times a trillion.

And now, here I am, being given the chance to write a cookbook. It's an opportunity to share some tried-and-true recipes that are personal and reader favorites, as well as share a whole load of new recipes for you to add to your arsenal!

So read on, friends. Get your measuring cups ready and make sure your sugar bowl is full. We have work to do.

MY RULES
(OR LACK THEREOF)
IN THE KITCHEN

Let's talk about my rules for being rule-less.

Since I am a home cook, taught by home cooks, I have an easy approach to most things kitchen related. But let's talk about where I draw the line. Beginning with butter.

❖ How I Do . . . ❖

BUTTER

Always use butter. Please. There is never an acceptable situation where margarine will do the trick. Trust me on this. I am the girl who grew up with a mother who had the big tub of I Can't Believe It's Not Butter! in the fridge at all times. I'm basically an expert on margarine. So you can be confident in knowing it's never okay.

Also, salted or unsalted? Oh, the question of the ages. I know lots of bakers and professional cooks use unsalted butter, and I certainly see the logic. Start with unsalted butter and you can control the exact amount of salt added to the recipe. Makes sense. However, I always use salted. #Sorrynotsorry. I just like it better, it's that simple. If you aren't a salty girl like me, go ahead and use unsalted and add a pinch or two of salt as you need. But please know I am always baking with salted butter, unless otherwise noted (which is pretty much never).

BAKEWARE

I'm a little picky about my baking sheets. The same dough, the same oven temperatures, the same everything . . . it won't matter. Different baking sheet, different results. It's a fact.

Think of it like this: The darker the baking sheet, the darker your cookies will get on the bottom. And also, the specific metal or thickness of certain baking sheets can drastically change the outcome of the cookie.

For example I very rarely, if ever, use insulated baking sheets for the reason that they don't produce browned edges. They might be great for a soft sugar cookie or shortbread that you don't want any darkness to, but for me that's about it.

I bake most often on light colored, basic aluminum or stainless steel baking sheets. Honestly my baking sheets are nothing fancy; they're light in color and weight and large (at least 14 x 17 inches)! I never bother with nonstick baking sheets either because I always, ALWAYS use parchment paper when baking cookies. I have tried the fancy silicone baking mats and nothing (in my opinion) beats classic parchment paper. Parchment makes the cleanup easy, but it also prevents sticking and bakes cookies evenly. Once you start baking with parchment you'll never go back.

The only time I use my silicone liners (like Silpat) is when I am baking something with an oozy caramel or a hard candy. Silicone is great for situations like those, because nothing will stick!

✣ Can't Live Without . . . ✣

MIXER

Obviously, I can't live without my KitchenAid stand mixer. I use it almost every day and it hasn't let me down yet. If you don't have a stand mixer, don't worry, although I would recommend adding it to your Christmas list next year. (What do you mean, kitchen tools aren't at the top of your holiday gift wish list? What's wrong with you?)

For the most part, a hand mixer will work fine, though it's not as powerful as a stand mixer because the motor just isn't as large. So for large batches of dough or thicker doughs, you could run into a problem . . . and in those cases you might want to divide and conquer.

MEASURING CUPS

Next up, if you do any baking I highly recommend a set of stainless steel measuring cups. The number of plastic sets

I have gone through only to break the handles off isn't even a joke. The metal ones aren't expensive, and in the long run will last pretty much forever. I am an avid brown sugar scooper, and have had many measuring-cup casualties in my brown sugar container. I guess if you have to die, it might be the way to go.

KOSHER SALT

Never again bake with table salt. Like I said before, I am a salty girl . . . but you will ABSOLUTELY oversalt the recipes in this book if you use the salt from your old-school shaker, as I developed and tested every recipe here using kosher salt. Table salt is a finer grain salt, so a 1-teaspoon measure holds way more fine grains than it does coarse grains. Make sense? It has nothing to do with the "kosher-ness" of it, it's all about the size of the grain.

BLENDER

I use a Blendtec, which is a very fancy expensive blender, so I get it if you just rolled your eyes at me. But it has taken the place of my food processor (which I loathe). I know, I know, lots of you love your processors, but I have found that a good blender with a quality motor is a great alternative. I use mine for making salsas, smoothies, frosting, nut butters, etc. I use it to chop things in a pinch and blend things when I am feeling lazy.

CAST-IRON SKILLET

I was a little late to the party with the cast-iron craze. My husband bought me one YEARS ago. I tried it, hated it, and never brought it out again until a few years back. The skillet he bought me was unseasoned, and I didn't give it a fair chance. We seasoned it according to the package directions, but that didn't cut the mustard. It took a few weeks of solid use, and now it's possibly the one thing in my kitchen, besides my mixer, that I couldn't live without. It's just a bonus that cast-iron skillets are pretty cheap, too! I make dinners, desserts, and everything in between in mine. It's a love affair.

❖ All About That Brand . . . ❖

I have to admit that I can be a bit picky about brands. Beyond shoes and purses, that brand loyalty extends to the kitchen. Also note that none of the brands I am listing here are paying me to promote them. These are all brands I love and purchase:

SUGAR: All the recipes in this book have been made with Imperial Sugar. It's a brand made in Sugarland, Texas, and I gotta support my state! Also, they make a great-quality sugar that has never disappointed.

KOSHER SALT: Morton Coarse Kosher Salt is the brand I always use and it's what I tested every recipe in this book with. I don't think it necessarily tastes any better than any other brand, but I wanted to make sure to include the brand, so there was no confusion.

COCONUT OIL: I am a huge fan of Carrington Farms unrefined coconut oil. It offers up a bit more coconut-y flavor than a refined oil, but I love it.

FLOUR: I use flour in pretty much everything I bake, obviously. As far as favorites go, I tend to stick with either King Arthur Flour or Gold Medal Flour. Both are great brands. I really like King Arthur Whole Wheat Flour. I sub that in chocolate chip cookies a LOT and it gives the cookies a subtle nutty flavor, which I love. I generally try to avoid store-brand flour, just based on results I have had in the past.

BUTTER: I am really a Challenge Dairy or Land O'Lakes girl. Unfortunately the Challenge brand isn't currently distributed in the Northeast (hope that changes), so when I am at my local New Jersey store I purchase Land O'Lakes. But if you live in an area where you can get Challenge, I HIGHLY recommend their European butter. OMG, you guys, it is life changing. European-style butter is a little pricier, but it has a higher fat/lower water content than everyday butter. Generally speaking, more fat = more delicious (and I agree in this case), so I mean, you do the math here. In most of your baked goods, like cookies and bar recipes, using European butter won't make a huge flavor difference, but in a cake or pastry it produces a richer, and in my opinion more delicious, result. Long story short, I'm a fan.

CHOCOLATE CHIPS: I use a TON of chocolate chips. My FAVORITE brand is Callebaut. I order it online or you can find it at Whole Foods. It's fancy shmancy, but it is perfection. I buy both the semisweet "mini chocolate chips" and "discs" to use in cookies, which turn out great. Callebaut calls their regular-size chips discs, as they are slightly flatter than normal chocolate chips. It's also a fantastic melting chocolate because it's ridiculously creamy.

I do also like Guittard and Scharffen Berger chocolate. I stock up on Guittard chips when I run across them, and Scharffen Berger is creamy dreamy and great for chocolate chunk cookies. But if you are looking for a solid everyday brand that is easy to find, I recommend Ghirardelli. Store-brand chocolate chips aren't great. Tough love, people, tough love.

❖ Tips, Tricks, and All the Kitchen Cheats I Know ❖

TO SIFT OR NOT TO SIFT

When I first started getting super serious about baking, I followed instructions down to every last detail.

Sift the dry ingredients? Oh, you betcha I did.

But now that I have been baking pretty nonstop for the last nine-ish years I have learned that there is definitely a time and a place for sifting. As a general

rule, when a recipe calls for a sift, you can pretty much get by with a whisk. Trust me on this.

Also, you will notice that in this book when I make cookies I rarely combine my dry ingredients separately from the wet. Nope. I'm a rebel like that.

I do, however, whisk my dry ingredients together first when making cakes. Cakes are more finicky, with their domes and their rising, and all the details. Cookies are way more forgiving, so take the cheat where you can.

If you happen to live in a very humid climate and your powdered sugar is all sorts of lumpy, then certainly grab that sifter out and get busy. But sifting is annoying to me, and I hate annoying things.

BROWNING BUTTER

The joy! I feel like most everything in life is exponentially more delicious with browned butter.

You'll see that I use browned butter a lot in this book, because it's way better in almost everything. Cookies? Check. Frosting? Checkity check. It's really a simple step that not only seems fancy (it isn't), but it makes everything you add it to nutty, rich, and just MORE.

Pretty much every time butter is used you can brown it.

The browning process is super-duper easy. I've explained it in most recipes in the book, but for a quick how-to, all you do is melt your butter over medium heat. Once it's melted, continue to cook the butter, bringing it to a boil. You will want to stir it or swirl the pan constantly, so the milk solids that separate don't burn. These milk solids that collect at the bottom of the pan will begin to brown, creating a nutty, rich flavor that can't be duplicated. When the butter is a deep amber color, remove it from the heat and allow it to cool before use. That's it!

I like to brown some butter and keep it in the fridge for whenever I need solid butter in a recipe. Trust me on this.

GREASED LIGHTNING

Let's talk about how to grease a cake pan.

I am a firm believer in cooking and baking sprays. I use them all the dang time. They're easy, effective, and quick. When I'm baking I like the sprays that contain flour as well; they're generally called baking sprays. When cooking, I use regular nonstick spray without the flour.

BUT. Don't feel like you HAVE to use baking spray. You don't.

In all the instances in this book that I use spray, you can grease the pan with butter or shortening instead. The only extra step that I do recommend in baking if you're going to go that route is to lightly dust it with flour as well. You obviously don't HAVE to, but it definitely helps with sticking. In that terrifying moment when you invert your pan and pray to the cake gods that your cake doesn't stick, you'll be glad you did.

DANG! I FORGOT TO SOFTEN MY BUTTER!

Don't fret, young one. It will be fine.

Clearly, allowing your butter to come to room temperature on its own is the best-case scenario, but when you're feeling a little murder-y and MUST HAVE A

COOKIE NOW for the sake of mankind, there is hope.

Using the microwave to warm the butter isn't ideal (and I'm not going to pretend I haven't done it a time or 300) because it melts unevenly. An easier way to get your butter ready without fear of that uneven melt is to cut it into small cubes and stick it in the bowl of a stand mixer. Beat that cold butter for about 2 minutes or so on medium speed until it is creamy. It works and your cookies will be fine. I swear it.

CAKE MIX . . . DO REAL BAKERS USE IT?

Let's all step down from our high horses right about now. You all KNOW you love a cake mix cake, don't front. The texture of cake mix cake is really the brass ring, something I have been trying to mimic for years. I have made my fair share of "scratch" cakes that my husband has eaten and said, "It's good, but your usual cake is better." And by "usual" he means Pillsbury. Trust me, I get it . . . the fluffi-ness, the perfect dome . . . boxes are sold by the millions for a reason.

And while I actually prefer the flavor of a homemade vanilla cake better, there are lots of folks out there who will dis-agree. It's cool.

So don't you let anyone make you feel like less of a baker because you open a box of cake mix. You're doing it, and that's all that matters.

What I WILL judge you on, friends, is if you use canned frosting. I feel like we're homies by now. And friends don't let friends peel back that foil lid. Please. Just don't do it.

Homemade frosting is way too easy to shortcut.

So go ahead and make your boxed cake. Just top it with some of my Perfect Buttercream (page 18) and be prepared for your friends to think you are a cake magician. You will quickly be known among all your nearest and dearest as The Cake Wizard. I know this, because I am this.

❖ part one ❖

DESSERT FIRST

---

*L*ike I mentioned in the introduction, this book is a cookbook in reverse. Oh wait, you didn't read the introduction? Yeah, you're gonna need to go back and do that real quick, 'kay?

Anyhow . . . desserts rule my life. And since we're already best friends I feel like you're with me on this. Too much too soon? Never.

I'm going to hit your sweet tooth up in the morning first and we're going to move on from there. I'm talking about cookies, brownies, cakes, and frosting. Party snacks and pie aren't to be forgotten, plus a whole section on treats you need to be the best at.

As my grandpa says, "Let's get this show on the road."

1

So You Think You Can Bake?

These are the recipes you need to nail.

*W*e all have our specialty in the kitchen, don't we? I mean, doesn't everyone think they make (or their mom makes) the best chicken noodle soup, the best chocolate chip cookies, the best whatever? Yep. And it's cool.

But if you don't already have "the best" recipe for some of the basics, I gotcha covered. You and me, we're ride or die.

P.S. *I* make the best chocolate chip cookies.

My Favorite Chocolate Chip Cookies

❧ Makes 24 cookies ❧

I feel like these cookies don't need any introduction. This recipe is the one that I have been making in my kitchen for years. It took a little bit of trial and error to develop, but once I got it I knew the search was over. These are big, buttery, and loaded with brown sugar and vanilla. I love to use mini chips in my cookies because I feel like you get more chocolate in every bite. You can easily use regular chips or even chunks if that's your thing, though. But the little detail in these cookies that sets them apart is the addition of coarse sea salt. It was an error my mom made in her chocolate chip cookies once, about 12 years ago. She meant to add regular salt and grabbed the coarse sea salt instead. Well, it was a revelation! The salty nuggets sprinkled throughout the cookie really make it special.

. . . .

1 cup (2 sticks) salted butter, at room temperature

¾ cup packed light brown sugar

¼ cup packed dark brown sugar

½ cup granulated sugar

2 large eggs

1 tablespoon vanilla extract

1 teaspoon baking soda

1 teaspoon baking powder

1 teaspoon coarse sea salt

2¾ cups all-purpose flour

1 (12-ounce) bag mini chocolate chips

1. In the bowl of a stand mixer fitted with the paddle attachment, beat the butter and all the sugars together on medium speed for 2 minutes until the butter is light and fluffy. Add the eggs and vanilla and continue mixing until smooth, scraping the sides of the bowl as necessary.

2. Add the baking soda, baking powder, and coarse sea salt. Mix until combined.

3. Turn the mixer speed to low and add the flour, mixing until incorporated.

4. Stir in the mini chocolate chips until evenly distributed. Cover the dough with plastic wrap and refrigerate it overnight or up to 48 hours.

5. When you're ready to bake, preheat the oven to 350°F. Line a baking sheet with parchment paper.

6. Using a large (3-tablespoon) cookie scoop, drop the dough 2 inches apart on the baking sheet.

7. Bake the cookies for 9 to 10 minutes, until the edges are golden brown and the centers are almost set. Underbaking the centers of the cookies slightly will help the cookies stay soft.

8. Allow the cookies to cool on the baking sheet for 3 to 4 minutes before transferring to a wire rack to cool completely.

Store airtight at room temperature for up to 3 days.

Classic Cut-Out Sugar Cookies

❖ Makes 24 large cookies ❖

*W*hen my official online baking adventure started back in 2008, my favorite cookie to make was a decorated sugar cookie. As the years have passed, I find myself making fewer decorated cookies, but I have to say they will probably always be my first love. This recipe for cut-out cookies produces the thickest, butteriest cookies that hold their shape perfectly, even with the most intricate of cutters. Chilling the dough helps greatly when you want crisply cut edges, so don't skip that step!

2 cups (4 sticks) salted butter, at room temperature

2 cups granulated sugar

2 large eggs

1 tablespoon vanilla extract

3 teaspoons baking powder

½ teaspoon kosher salt

6 cups all-purpose flour

1. Line baking sheets with parchment paper.

2. In the bowl of a stand mixer fitted with the paddle attachment, beat the butter and sugar together on medium speed for 2 minutes until light and fluffy.

3. Add the eggs and the vanilla and continue mixing until combined and smooth, scraping the sides of the bowl as necessary.

4. Turn the mixer speed to low and add the baking powder, salt, and flour, mixing until the dough comes together.

5. Divide the dough into 3 portions. On a floured work surface, roll the dough to ⅓ inch thick. Using cookie cutters, cut out your desired shapes and place the cookies 1½ inches apart on the prepared baking sheets. Re-roll the leftover dough scraps and repeat the process, using all the dough.

6. Place the baking sheets in the refrigerator for 20 to 30 minutes to chill the dough.

7. Meanwhile, preheat the oven to 350°F.

8. Bake the chilled cookies for 8 to 10 minutes, until the edges are lightly golden.

9. Allow the cookies to cool on the baking sheet for 5 minutes, then transfer to a wire rack to cool completely.

Store airtight at room temperature for up to 5 days.

Tips: You can chill the dough before cutting the cookies out as well. Just chill the dough for at least 2 hours before rolling and cutting. Keep the unused portion in the refrigerator until ready to use.

I use my Glaze Icing (page 171) on top of these for a sweet finish, but really, you can use any type of frosting!

The Fudgiest Brownies

❧ Makes 24 large brownies ❧

*O*kay, sure, I fall into the trap of boxed brownie mixes. I will be the first to admit that there are a few brands out there that nail the brownie game. But folks, if you truly want the richest, fudgiest brownie out there, make them from scratch. This recipe is everything you could possibly want in a fudgy brownie. I'm talking stick-to-your-teeth fudgy. Using melted chocolate instead of cocoa powder in the recipe makes these the softest, most chocolaty brownies you will ever try. They are super easy, are made in one pot, and bake to perfection. This will be your go-to brownie recipe for sure!

1 cup semisweet chocolate chips

1 cup milk chocolate chips

½ cup (1 stick) salted butter

¾ cup packed light brown sugar

¾ cup granulated sugar

4 large eggs

2 teaspoons vanilla extract

½ teaspoon kosher salt

1 cup all-purpose flour

1. Preheat the oven to 325°F. Line a 9 x 13-inch baking pan with foil and coat generously with cooking spray.

2. In a medium saucepan, combine the semisweet chips, milk chocolate chips, and butter and melt over medium-low heat, stirring constantly. Once the chocolate is melted, remove the pan from the heat immediately.

3. Whisk both of the sugars into the chocolate and add the eggs, one at a time, whisking constantly, until evenly combined. Next mix in the vanilla until smooth. Stir in the salt and flour until they're evenly incorporated and pour the batter into the prepared pan.

4. Bake the brownies for 35 to 40 minutes, until the center is set and a toothpick inserted 3 inches in from the edge comes out clean.

5. Let the brownies cool completely in the pan before cutting into 24 bars.

Store airtight at room temperature for up to 3 days.

Tip: You can use any combination of chocolate chips in this recipe. If you prefer a darker chocolate brownie, use all semisweet chocolate. If you prefer a sweeter, lighter brownie, use all milk chocolate.

Gooey Marshmallow Krispie Treats

*T*his is the recipe that you never knew you needed. We all grew up on the popular marshmallow bar. My mom used the recipe on the side of the Rice Krispies box, which is fantastic. And as I grew up, Krispie Treats remained one of my most favorite indulgences. My recipe takes the original and makes it lighter and gooier with just a few simple tricks. Once you start making Krispie Treats with my recipe, you'll never go back!

5 tablespoons salted butter

10 cups mini marshmallows

½ teaspoon vanilla extract

½ teaspoon kosher salt

6 cups Rice Krispies cereal

1. Line a 9 x 9-inch pan with foil and coat lightly with cooking spray.

2. In a large pot, melt the butter over low heat. Once the butter is melted, add 8 cups of the mini marshmallows, stirring constantly.

3. Once the marshmallows are just melted, remove immediately from the heat and stir in the vanilla and salt until combined. Next add the cereal and stir until just coated in marshmallow mixture. Finally, stir in the remaining 2 cups mini marshmallows.

4. Pour the mixture into the prepared pan and press evenly (see Tip). Allow to cool completely before cutting into squares.

These are best served the same day, but they can be stored airtight at room temperature for up to 2 days.

Tip: Use a piece of parchment or wax paper coated lightly with cooking spray to help press the mixture into the pan to avoid sticky bits all over your fingers!

Vanilla Bean Snickerdoodles

❧ Makes 30 cookies ❧

*S*nickerdoodles are my husband's most favorite cookie. I know he's not alone . . . people have very serious opinions on snickerdoodles and since I run a food blog I have heard my fair share. But after years of making *Better Homes and Gardens'* version (which is a classic, by the way), I decided to take the bull by the horns and come up with my own recipe, one that's a little softer, a little more cinnamony, and PACKED with vanilla. I am pretty sure these will be on your permanent rotation!

1 cup (2 sticks) salted butter, at room temperature

¾ cup granulated sugar

½ cup packed light brown sugar

1 large egg

1 egg yolk

2 teaspoons vanilla extract

2 vanilla beans

1 teaspoon ground cinnamon

1 teaspoon baking soda

1 teaspoon cream of tartar

½ teaspoon kosher salt

2¾ cups all-purpose flour

CINNAMON SUGAR:

¼ cup granulated sugar

1 tablespoon ground cinnamon

1. Preheat the oven to 350°F. Line a baking sheet with parchment paper.

2. In the bowl of a stand mixer fitted with the paddle attachment, beat the butter and both sugars together on medium speed for 2 minutes, scraping the sides of the bowl as necessary.

3. Add the whole egg, egg yolk, and vanilla extract. Mix until smooth.

4. Using a sharp knife, split the vanilla beans in half lengthwise and use the tip of the knife to scrape all the vanilla seeds out of the pod and into the bowl. Mix until combined. Add the cinnamon, baking soda, cream of tartar, and salt and mix on medium speed until evenly incorporated.

5. Turn the mixer speed to low and beat in the flour until the dough comes together.

6. *For the cinnamon sugar:* In a small bowl, whisk together the granulated sugar and cinnamon.

7. Using a medium (2-tablespoon) cookie scoop, portion out the dough, roll into balls, and then roll each ball in the cinnamon sugar mixture, coating evenly.

8. Place the balls 2 inches apart on the baking sheet. Bake for 10 to 12 minutes, until the edges are lightly golden, rotating the baking sheet front to back halfway through baking. The tops may seem slightly underbaked, but this is okay.

9. Transfer the cookies to a wire rack to cool completely.

Store airtight at room temperature for up to 3 days.

Brown Sugar Blondies

❧ Makes 20 blondies ❧

*W*hile I do love brownies, my heart belongs to the blondie. This buttery, brown sugar bar is perfectly sweet with a mild caramel taste. You can play around with what you add in. For instance, if you like nuts, go for it! But I prefer the addition of toasted coconut and chocolate chips. The coconut adds a hint of toasty sweetness, and even people who say they don't like coconut will eat these and never be the wiser. Also, I like to brown the butter before baking these to add a deep nutty flavor that can't be topped.

1 cup (2 sticks) salted butter

¾ cup sweetened flaked coconut

2 cups packed light brown sugar

1 large egg

1 egg yolk

1 tablespoon vanilla extract

1 teaspoon baking powder

1 teaspoon coarse sea salt

2 cups all-purpose flour

1 cup semisweet or milk chocolate chips

1. Preheat the oven to 350°F. Line a 9 x 13-inch baking pan with foil and coat the foil with cooking spray.

2. In a medium saucepan, melt the butter over medium heat, then bring it to a boil. Once it starts boiling, swirl the pan constantly until the butter passes the foamy phase and becomes a deep amber color. Remove from the heat and allow the butter to cool for 20 minutes.

3. In a medium skillet, toast the coconut flakes over medium heat until lightly golden, stirring frequently. Once they begin to get golden in color, watch carefully as they will burn quickly. Remove from the heat as soon as they are lightly toasted and set aside.

4. In the bowl of a stand mixer fitted with the paddle attachment, beat the butter and brown sugar together on low speed until evenly combined.

5. With the mixer still on low, add the whole egg, egg yolk, and vanilla and mix until evenly incorporated. Beat in the baking powder and salt, then beat in the flour until just combined.

6. Stir in the chocolate chips and toasted coconut, either by hand or with the mixer on its lowest setting.

7. Spread the batter into the prepared pan and bake for 20 to 25 minutes, until the center is no longer shiny and a toothpick inserted 3 inches from the edge comes out clean.

8. Allow the bars to cool completely in the pan before cutting into squares.

Store airtight at room temperature for up to 3 days.

Tip: You can also bake these in a 9 x 9-inch baking pan if you prefer a thicker blondie. You will need to adjust the baking time to 25 to 30 minutes.

The Essential Vanilla Cake

*E*veryone needs a solid vanilla cake in their baking arsenal. It has to be buttery, soft, and loaded with vanilla flavor. It's the perfect cake for just about anything you'd like to top it with. Don't wait for a party to make this cake—this cake brings the party all on its own!

3 cups all-purpose flour

2 teaspoons baking powder

½ teaspoon kosher salt

1 cup (2 sticks) salted butter, at room temperature

2 cups granulated sugar

¼ cup vegetable oil

4 large eggs

1 tablespoon vanilla extract

1 cup whole milk

1. Preheat the oven to 350°F. Coat three 8-inch or two 9-inch round cake pans with cooking spray. Line the bottoms of the pans with rounds of parchment paper. Coat the pan sides and parchment with cooking spray.

2. In a medium bowl, whisk together the flour, baking powder, and salt. Set aside.

3. In the bowl of a stand mixer fitted with the paddle attachment, beat the butter and sugar together on medium speed for 2 minutes. Add the oil, eggs, and vanilla and continue mixing until smooth, scraping the sides of the bowl as necessary.

4. Turn the mixer to low and add one-third of the flour mixture, followed by half of the milk, beating after each addition. Repeat this step. End with a final addition of the flour mixture. Turn the mixer up to medium and mix for 30 seconds.

5. Divide the batter equally among the pans.

6. Bake for 25 to 30 minutes, until the centers are set and a toothpick inserted into the middle of a cake comes out clean.

7. Allow the cakes to cool in the pans for 5 minutes, then invert them onto a wire rack to cool completely.

Tip: Top it with my Creamy Chocolate Frosting (page 155) for a classic cake, or mix things up and slather it with any of the fun frostings I have in chapter 6, Frosting!

Perfect Buttercream

What would this book be without buttercream? Frosting can make or break a cake, and there is no excuse for subpar frosting . . . not when my recipe for it is so easy. This simple buttercream is buttery, creamy, and spreadable, but it also works great for piping high swirls or even roses if you're fancy! You can toss some peanut butter into it and you have peanut butter frosting; you can add some Nutella and have Nutella frosting . . . in other words, it's ridiculously adaptable and basically impossible to mess up. Oh yeah, and it's also outrageously delicious!

1 cup (2 sticks) salted butter, at room temperature

½ cup solid vegetable shortening (such as Crisco)

7 cups powdered sugar

¼ to ⅓ cup heavy cream

1 teaspoon vanilla extract

1. In the bowl of a stand mixer fitted with the paddle attachment, beat the butter and shortening together on medium speed until smooth. Turn the speed to low and slowly add the powdered sugar until it's mixed in.

2. Slowly stream in ¼ cup of the heavy cream and the vanilla. Turn the mixer up to medium speed and mix for 1 minute until creamy. Add additional heavy cream if you prefer a creamier frosting.

Store airtight in the refrigerator for up to 1 week, or in the freezer for 1 month. Allow the frosting to come to room temperature before using.

All-Butter Pie Dough

❧ *Makes enough for 2 crusts for 9-inch pie* ❧

I have always been scared of pie crust. My mom was a great pie maker and taught me her tricks years ago, always insisting that it was so easy. While I certainly believed her, it just seemed easier to use a premade crust . . . or even better, just have her make the pie! After she passed away a few years ago I decided to pull her recipe out and give it a go on my own. While I can never seem to make my pies look as pretty as hers, I am pretty confident she would approve!

· ·

2½ cups all-purpose flour

2 tablespoons light brown sugar

1 teaspoon kosher salt

1 cup (2 sticks) cold salted butter (frozen works too), cubed or grated

2 teaspoons apple cider vinegar

½ to ¾ cup ice water

1. In a large metal bowl, whisk together the flour, brown sugar, and salt.

2. Add the cold cubed or grated butter to the flour mixture and use a pastry cutter or a fork to combine the butter with the flour until it resembles coarse sand.

3. Add the vinegar and ½ cup ice water and stir until it becomes too difficult, at which point use your hands, working quickly to knead the dough until it holds together. It should not be sticky; however, if the dough is too dry or crumbles apart, add 1 tablespoon more water at a time until the dough holds together.

4. Divide the dough in half and form each portion into a flat disc. Wrap each portion with plastic wrap and refrigerate for at least 1 hour and up to 3 days.

5. When you are ready to use the dough, roll out on a lightly floured surface to a 13-inch round. Fit the rolled-out dough into a pie plate, trim, and pinch the edges to form a decorative rim.

6. *To prebake a crust:* Preheat the oven to 375°F.

7. After fitting the dough into the pie plate, place the plate in the freezer for at least 30 minutes.

8. Cut out a round of parchment paper the same diameter as the bottom of the pie shell and place into the frozen crust. Top this with pie weights or dried beans.

9. Bake the crust for 15 minutes. Remove from the oven and remove the weights and the parchment round. Return to the oven to bake for 10 to 15 minutes longer, until the crust is golden. If the edges of the crust begin to brown too much, use a pie crust shield or strips of foil to cover the edges and continue baking.

Tips: *Keep your butter as cold as possible, only pulling it out of the refrigerator right when you're ready to use it. I really like to freeze my butter and then grate it quickly—that way it combines easily without my having to handle the dough very much. Your hands warm the butter fast, which is why I like to use my pastry cutter as much as possible to mix the dough. Handling it less leaves little pockets of butter, which helps produce a flakier crust.*

You can also freeze your dough before using it. Simply store it wrapped and in an airtight container for up to a month, allowing it to thaw before rolling it out.

If you are prebaking your crust, you can prick the pie crust with a fork on the bottom and sides prior to baking. This method is only necessary if you are not using pie weights (see Step 8).

Eat Cake for Breakfast!

And other remedies for the morning sweet tooth.

2

Long gone are the days where I try to justify eating leftover birthday cake for breakfast. There once was a time when I thought this was behavior that needed explaining. While I certainly appreciate the art of a good omelet, there isn't anything much better than a sweet treat at eight a.m. I mean, if Pop-Tarts and Fruity Pebbles are acceptable breakfast foods, I do believe a giant blueberry muffin shouldn't garner any strange glances. And we all know a muffin is basically just a cupcake without the frosting, so . . .

Brown Sugar Cinnamon Swirl Bread

❧ Serves 8 ❧

$\mathcal{I}$ am all about eating cake for breakfast. So I would like to high-five whoever invented quick bread, which is basically cake baked in a loaf pan. And apparently cake in a loaf pan is breakfast-acceptable. Not sure the hows or whys of that, but I'm not going to argue with clear genius. This bread/cake is insanely moist, rich with brown sugar, and swirled with the perfect amount of cinnamon. There won't be a slice left, I guarantee it!

SWIRL MIXTURE:

½ cup (1 stick) salted butter, at room temperature

½ cup packed light brown sugar

1 tablespoon all-purpose flour

1 tablespoon ground cinnamon

BREAD:

2 cups all-purpose flour

1 teaspoon baking soda

½ teaspoon kosher salt

1 large egg

1 cup packed light brown sugar

1 cup buttermilk (*see DIY option*)

⅓ cup vegetable or canola oil

1 tablespoon vanilla extract

GLAZE:

2 tablespoons salted butter, melted

1 cup powdered sugar

2 to 3 tablespoons heavy cream

1. Preheat the oven to 350°F. Coat a 9 x 5-inch loaf pan with cooking spray. Place a long strip of parchment paper cut to fit the width of the pan in the bottom of the pan and up the two short ends to use to lift the bread out of the pan after it's baked. Coat the parchment paper with cooking spray.

2. *For the swirl mixture:* In a medium bowl, mix the butter, brown sugar, flour, and cinnamon together until evenly combined. Set aside.

3. *For the bread:* In a large bowl, whisk the flour, baking soda, and salt. In another large bowl, whisk together the egg, brown sugar, buttermilk, oil, and vanilla. Add the flour mixture to the wet ingredients and stir until smooth.

4. Pour two-thirds of the batter into the prepared pan. Drop half of the swirl mixture, by the teaspoon, onto the batter. Top this with the remaining batter and finally the remaining swirl mixture. With a butter knife carefully swirl the batter and swirl mixture together.

5. Bake for 50 to 60 minutes, until the center is set and a toothpick inserted into the center comes out clean.

6. Allow it to cool in the pan for 10 to 15 minutes, then using the exposed parchment paper, carefully remove it from the pan onto a plate or wire rack.

7. *For the glaze:* In a small bowl, whisk together the melted butter, powdered sugar, and cream (use the amount of cream you want to get the consistency you prefer). Drizzle the glaze on top of the warm bread.

8. Serve warm or at room temperature.

Store airtight at room temperature for up to 3 days.

Buttermilk

❧ *Makes 1 cup* ❧

I am consistently out of buttermilk. It's not an ingredient I use on a daily basis . . . and the fact that it's perishable means I need to plan better or heck, just make my own. This little trick is a pretty great sub-in for any recipe that calls for buttermilk. Of course using fresh buttermilk is ideal, but this fake it 'til you make it cheat is the next best option.

1 cup 2% or whole milk

4 teaspoons distilled white
    vinegar or lemon juice

1. Stir the milk and the vinegar (or lemon juice) together. Allow the mixture to sit for at least 5 minutes. It will curdle slightly, this is okay. Use whenever your recipe calls for buttermilk.

2. Store airtight in the refrigerator for up to 5 days.

Perfect Waffles

I save my waffle-making for weekend breakfasts. I wish I could be that mom who gets up early and makes eggs, pancakes, and waffles for my kids before school . . . but I learned to accept my limitations many years ago. School days are oatmeal, cereal, and the occasional "egg-in-a-basket." But weekends = waffles. It took a while to get me to think outside the Bisquick box when it came to waffle-making. But once I made the leap, there was no going back. This recipe has egg whites that are folded into the batter, creating a crispy outside and a soft inside, just the way a waffle should be!

2 cups all-purpose flour

½ teaspoon kosher salt

4 teaspoons baking powder

2 large eggs, separated

1 teaspoon vanilla extract

1 tablespoon brown sugar

½ cup canola oil

1¾ cups whole or 2% milk, warmed

Syrup, for serving

1. Heat a waffle iron and coat lightly with cooking spray.

2. In a large bowl, whisk together the flour, salt, and baking powder.

3. In another large bowl, whisk together the egg yolks, vanilla, brown sugar, and oil. Alternate adding the flour mixture and warm milk to the egg yolk mixture, beginning and ending with the flour mixture. Mix until smooth.

4. In the bowl of a stand mixer fitted with the whisk attachment, beat the egg whites until stiff peaks form. Fold the egg whites into the waffle batter until just combined.

5. Scoop ¾ cup of the batter into the hot waffle iron and cook until golden brown.

6. Serve immediately with syrup.

Tips: *I regularly sub in coconut oil for the canola oil in this recipe. Just make sure that you measure the coconut oil in its liquid state, not solid.*

Another switch I make occasionally is to replace 1 cup of the all-purpose flour with 1 cup of whole wheat flour. Combining the all-purpose with the whole wheat flour makes a nice textured waffle with a bit of a nutty flavor that I love.

Also, I generally just warm the milk for 30 seconds in the microwave. You could definitely do it on the stovetop if you prefer, but only heat it until it's warm to the touch, not hot.

The Essential Blueberry Streusel Muffin

❖ *Makes 12 muffins* ❖

*B*lueberry muffins are one of those treats that everyone just loves. With such a sentimental and nostalgic food, most everyone has his or her own recipe, whether it be one passed down from your grandma, or one that you have come up with on your own. For so many years the perfect blueberry muffin eluded me. I just couldn't get it right . . . which in my world means overreactions consisting of cuss words, trashed muffins, and tears. They were either too dense, too crumbly, too dry, or too oily. But after much trial and error I nailed it. In my opinion, you won't find a better blueberry muffin out there. Mine are fluffy, soft, loaded with blueberries, and topped with crunchy crumb topping! This muffin is a total babe.

MUFFINS:

1½ cups all-purpose flour

1½ teaspoons baking powder

½ teaspoon kosher salt

6 tablespoons salted butter, at room temperature

½ cup granulated sugar

¾ cup sour cream

1 large egg

1 teaspoon vanilla extract

1 cup blueberries, fresh or thawed frozen

STREUSEL TOPPING:

4 tablespoons (½ stick) cold salted butter, cubed

½ cup packed light brown sugar

½ cup all-purpose flour

1. Preheat the oven to 350°F. Line 12 cups of a muffin tin with paper liners or coat liberally with cooking spray.

2. *For the muffins:* In a medium bowl, whisk together the flour, baking powder, and salt. Set aside.

3. In the bowl of a stand mixer fitter with the paddle attachment, beat the butter and granulated sugar together on medium speed for 2 minutes. Add the sour cream, egg, and vanilla and beat until smooth, scraping the sides of the bowl as necessary.

4. Turn the mixer speed to low and beat in the flour mixture until just combined. The batter will be fairly thick. Stir in the blueberries.

5. Fill each muffin cup two-thirds full with batter. Set the pan aside while you make the streusel topping.

6. *For the streusel topping:* In a bowl, combine the butter, brown sugar, and flour and blend with a pastry cutter or fork until evenly incorporated. Then, using your hands, form the mixture into crumbs.

7. Dividing evenly, sprinkle the streusel topping over the muffin batter and bake for 20 to 25 minutes, until the muffins are set and lightly golden.

8. Allow the muffins to cool in the pan for 5 minutes and then remove from the pan.

9. Serve warm or at room temperature.

Store airtight at room temperature for up to 2 days.

Banana Bread Pancakes

❧ Makes 18 (4-inch) pancakes ❧

J have never been a great pancake maker. They're basically my kitchen kryptonite. I either flip them too early and splatter batter from here to kingdom come, or I flip them too late and burn one side. Usually in that case, I flip them to the best side and try to trick my kids into eating them. Unfortunately they have gotten fairly pancake savvy and check both sides before accepting the plate. I can't say I blame them. Anyhow, I made it my mission to learn the art of pancakery. And not only to learn the art but to *raise* the pancake bar. Go big or go home, right? Slather them with butter and drizzle them with syrup, or eat them plain, you really can't go wrong! And I have to say, low and slow is the way to cook them! Enjoy!

1½ cups all-purpose flour

1½ cups whole wheat flour

4 teaspoons baking powder

½ teaspoon kosher salt

½ teaspoon ground cinnamon

2 very ripe medium bananas, mashed

2 teaspoons vanilla extract

⅓ cup vegetable oil

3 large eggs, beaten

2 cups milk (preferably 2% or whole)

¼ cup packed light brown sugar

Salted or unsalted butter, for frying the pancakes

1. In a large bowl, whisk together both flours, the baking powder, salt, and cinnamon.

2. In a separate bowl, mix together the bananas, vanilla, oil, eggs, milk, and brown sugar. Add the banana mixture into the flour mixture and stir until combined. The batter will be slightly lumpy.

3. Heat a large skillet or griddle over medium-low heat. When the skillet is hot, melt ½ tablespoon of butter on the skillet. Portion out ⅓ cup batter and pour onto the hot pan. Flip the pancakes over when bubbles start to form on the tops and the edges are set. Continue cooking until the pancakes are golden brown, adding more butter to the pan for each batch.

Tips: We serve these pancakes warm with maple syrup and sometimes top them with sliced bananas.

I like to make a large batch of these at the beginning of the week and let my kids heat them up in the morning for breakfast before school.

OMG Pull-Apart Praline Bread

❖ Serves 8 ❖

*I*f you make nothing else from this book (make everything), please, please make this bread. As you know already from the introduction (if you haven't read it, go now—I'll wait), monkey bread holds a special place in my heart, as it is a recipe that I used to make all the time with my grandma. I knew I wanted to include a version of the popular breakfast treat in my book for sure, but I wanted to switch up my grandma's recipe a bit. I started with homemade yeast dough, and that alteration alone takes this to a whole new level. On top of that I covered the whole darn thing in a glorious brown sugar icing that you will dream about. I'm telling ya, this one is a keeper.

DOUGH:

1 (¼-ounce) envelope active dry yeast (2¼ teaspoons)

1 teaspoon granulated sugar

1⅓ cups warm water (not above 110°F)

3½ to 4 cups all-purpose flour

2 teaspoons kosher salt

2 tablespoons vegetable oil

COATING:

¾ cup chopped pecans

1¼ cups packed light brown sugar

½ cup (1 stick) salted butter, melted

ICING:

4 tablespoons (½ stick) salted butter

1 cup packed light brown sugar

¼ cup heavy cream

1 cup powdered sugar

1. *For the dough:* In a small bowl, mix together the yeast, granulated sugar, and warm water and allow the mixture to sit for 4 minutes until the yeast is dissolved.

2. In the bowl of a stand mixer fitted with the dough hook, mix 3½ cups flour, the salt, and oil together on low speed. Stir the yeast mixture to combine, then slowly add it to the bowl with the flour. Mix this on medium speed for 5 to 6 minutes. If the dough is excessively sticky, add the remaining flour 1 tablespoon at a time until it becomes smooth.

3. Coat the inside of a large bowl with cooking spray and transfer the dough to the bowl. Cover with a clean kitchen towel and allow it to rise for 2 to 3 hours at room temperature until doubled in size. (Or place in the refrigerator and allow the dough to rise overnight, see Tip.)

4. Preheat the oven to 350°F.

5. *For the coating:* Coat a Bundt or tube pan with cooking spray. Evenly sprinkle half of the pecans into the bottom of the pan.

6. In a small bowl, stir together the brown sugar and melted butter.

7. Punch the risen dough down and tear pieces of the dough off and roll into 1-inch balls. Dip each dough ball into the brown sugar/butter mixture and place in the prepared pan. Continue this with all the dough, placing it in the pan evenly. Drizzle any remaining brown sugar/butter mixture on top of the dough and finally sprinkle on the remaining pecans.

8. Bake the bread for 30 to 35 minutes, until it's risen and lightly golden.

9. Remove the pan from the oven and place on a wire rack to cool slightly.

10. *Meanwhile, for the icing:* In a medium saucepan, combine the butter, brown sugar, and heavy cream and cook, stirring frequently, until it comes to a boil. Boil for 1 minute, then immediately remove from the heat and whisk in the powdered sugar.

11. Invert the Bundt pan onto a cake stand or serving platter. Drizzle the icing evenly on top of the bread. Serve warm.

Store airtight at room temperature for up to a day.

Tip: I like to place my dough in a gallon-size zip-top bag (coated with cooking spray) and refrigerate it overnight. This works great because in the cooler temperature the dough rises more slowly, letting you make the dough further in advance. You get the same results and the dough is ready in the morning for breakfast!

Ice Cream–Soaked French Toast

❖ Serves 6 ❖

*T*his idea is so smart, isn't it? Unfortunately I can't say that I came up with it. I was on a fun girls' trip to Seaside, Florida, a few years ago and we had the pleasure of eating breakfast at a little place called Pickles. I ordered the French toast, and it was literally one of the best things I have ever eaten. The sweet owner named Heavenly—yes, that is her real name—told us that her secret was soaking the French toast in ice cream. It was the most genius idea I had ever heard, and I knew I needed to try it! While she wouldn't give up her exact recipe, I think I came pretty darn close. If you are ever in Seaside you definitely need to stop by Pickles and order that French toast!

. . . .

1 cup vanilla ice cream, melted

4 eggs, beaten

¼ teaspoon ground cinnamon

12 slices Texas toast

6 tablespoons (½ stick) salted or unsalted butter

1. In a shallow bowl, combine the ice cream, eggs, and cinnamon.

2. Heat a skillet over medium heat.

3. Working with 1 slice at a time, dip the bread in the egg mixture and allow it to soak for 15 seconds on each side, until the bread has absorbed the mixture but is not completely saturated.

4. Melt ½ tablespoon butter in the hot skillet, then place a slice of the soaked bread onto the skillet. Cook the bread until it is lightly golden on both sides, 2 to 3 minutes per side.

5. Repeat this process with all the bread and serve hot.

Tip: If you can't find Texas toast in your area, just use any other bread that is sliced slightly thicker. Challah or brioche would be fantastic in this recipe. Just stay away from any bread that is too dense.

Pumpkin Crumb Cake

❖ Serves 12 ❖

J never thought I was a fan of pumpkin. I blame this on the Pilgrims, of course. Every year when Thanksgiving would roll around, my mom would make a huge variety of pies: pumpkin, lemon meringue, chocolate chip . . . but as a kid, I considered pumpkin to be a vegetable (even though I now know it's actually a fruit), and vegetables had no business being in my dessert. Pass the chocolate chip pie, please!

As I got older I carried my "no pumpkin" rule with me pretty closely. That is, until I was introduced to the very basic pumpkin spice latte. And being the super cliché woman I am, pumpkin suddenly became a thing in my life. Which, in the most roundabout way possible, has brought me to the point . . . Pumpkin Crumb Cake. It's rich and soft and topped with a buttery streusel.

So the moral of the story is, you can thank Starbucks for this recipe.

. . . .

CAKE:

2 cups all-purpose flour

2½ teaspoons baking powder

1 teaspoon kosher salt

1½ teaspoons pumpkin pie spice (*see DIY option*)

½ cup (1 stick) salted butter, at room temperature

2 cups granulated sugar

2 large eggs

1 tablespoon vanilla extract

1 (15-ounce) can unsweetened pumpkin puree

1 cup whole milk

CRUMB TOPPING:

½ cup (1 stick) cold salted butter, cubed

1 cup packed light brown sugar

1½ cups all-purpose flour

½ teaspoon kosher salt

1. Preheat the oven to 350°F. Coat a 9 x 13-inch baking dish with cooking spray.

2. *For the cake:* In a large bowl, whisk together the flour, baking powder, salt, and pumpkin pie spice. Set aside.

3. In the bowl of a stand mixer fitted with the paddle attachment, mix the butter and sugar on medium speed until combined, 1 to 2 minutes. Add the eggs, vanilla, and pumpkin, mixing until smooth, scraping the sides of the bowl as necessary.

4. Turn the speed to low and add one-third of the flour mixture and then half of the milk, beating well after each addition. Repeat this process. End with a final addition of the remaining flour. Turn the mixer back up to medium and mix for 1 more minute until the batter is smooth, scraping the sides of the bowl as necessary.

5. Spread the batter evenly in the prepared pan.

6. *For the crumb:* To make the crumb mixture, cut together the butter, brown sugar, flour, and salt using a pastry cutter or a fork until combined. Use your hands to form the mixture into medium-size crumbs and spread the crumb mixture on top of the cake batter.

7. Bake for 45 to 55 minutes, until the center is set and a toothpick inserted in the middle comes out clean.

8. Serve warm or at room temperature.

Store airtight at room temperature for up to 3 days.

Pumpkin Pie Spice

❧ *Makes ¼ cup* ❧

*P*umpkin pie spice is one of those spice mixtures that you should really replace every year. Generally we use all of it in the fall when pumpkin baking is in full swing. There have been SO many times that I have started a recipe only to realize I am out! Luckily it's a really easy one to throw together with items you most likely already have.

2 tablespoons ground cinnamon

1 tablespoon ground ginger

1½ teaspoons ground cloves

1 teaspoon ground allspice

1 teaspoon ground nutmeg

¼ teaspoon citric acid (optional)

In a small bowl, combine the cinnamon, ginger, cloves, allspice, nutmeg, and citric acid (if using) and mix until evenly distributed. Store airtight for up to 3 months.

Honey and Brown Sugar Baked Oatmeal

❖ Serves 4 ❖

My boys love oatmeal, but I will tell you that those little packets of the instant version don't go a long way, plus they're pretty pricey. There are mornings where I see each of them pulling out 2 or 3 packets just to fill their tummies! And then, of course, there are the variety boxes where one odd flavor is left that no one will touch (I'm looking at you, Peaches and Cream). To solve this monetary crisis in my house I started buying plain oatmeal in bulk and doctoring it up with brown sugar and spices. I also played around with ways to cook the oats, and the first time I baked my oatmeal I knew it was a game changer. First, it's super easy, and second, it's 1,000 times more delicious! I like to use honey in mine, but you could easily sub in maple syrup. The great thing about this recipe is that you can mix in your favorite extras like raisins (or any dried fruit), shredded coconut, cinnamon, chocolate chips, or even nuts! Play around with it and make it your own.

3 cups old-fashioned rolled oats

¾ cup packed dark brown sugar

2 teaspoons baking powder

½ teaspoon kosher salt

1 cup 2% or whole milk, plus more for serving

½ cup unsweetened applesauce

¼ cup honey

2 teaspoons vanilla extract

4 tablespoons (½ stick) salted butter, melted

1. Preheat the oven to 350°F. Grease an 8 x 8-inch baking dish with butter.

2. In a large bowl, mix together the oats, brown sugar, baking powder, salt, milk, applesauce, honey, and vanilla, stirring to combine evenly.

3. Pour the mixture into the prepared pan and then drizzle the melted butter on top.

4. Bake for 35 to 40 minutes until the center is set.

5. Serve warm and drizzle more milk on top, if desired.

Tip: You can use coconut milk in place of the dairy milk in this recipe to add another layer of flavor.

Cereal Squares

*T*hese quick squares are infinitely adaptable, and perfect for an on-the-go breakfast or snack. You can use any combination of cereals you prefer, with any type of dried fruit you like! I sometimes even add pumpkin seeds or nuts into the mixture to make the squares a little heartier. Recipes that allow you to use your own imagination are my favorite!

- -

1 cup quick-cooking oats

1½ cups lightly crushed cornflakes

1 cup chopped dried fruit, like raisins

1½ cups Cheerios

2½ cups Rice Krispies cereal

4 tablespoons (½ stick) salted butter

10 ounces mini marshmallows

1. Line a 9 x 13-inch baking dish with foil and coat lightly with cooking spray.

2. In a skillet, brown the oats over medium heat until lightly toasted, stirring frequently. Remove from the heat, scrape into a bowl, and set aside to cool.

3. Add the cornflakes, dried fruit, Cheerios, and Rice Krispies to the bowl with the oats.

4. In a large saucepan, melt the butter over low heat. Add the marshmallows and stir constantly until melted. Remove the pan from the heat and stir the oat and cereal mixture into the marshmallows, coating evenly.

5. Press the mixture evenly into the prepared pan and allow it to cool before cutting into squares.

Store airtight at room temperature for up to 3 days.

Toffee-Speckled Banana Bread

❖ Serves 6 ❖

*B*anana bread is one of those foods in my house that just feels like home. Everyone's mom has a recipe for banana bread, and everyone's mom makes the BEST banana bread. Luckily I am a mom, which I guess means I must make the best, too! I like to switch this recipe up occasionally, sometimes adding chocolate chips, sometimes peanut butter cups, and sometimes I just make it (gasp!) plain. But my favorite addition is toffee bits. The toffee adds a subtle sweetness and caramel flavor that complements the bananas perfectly, in my opinion. Served warm there might not be anything better. Except when it's served warm with butter.

½ cup (1 stick) salted butter, at room temperature

1 cup packed light brown sugar

¼ cup whole milk

2 large eggs

2 teaspoons vanilla extract

1½ cups mashed bananas (about 3 large very ripe bananas)

2 teaspoons baking powder

1 teaspoon kosher salt

2 cups all-purpose flour

1 cup toffee bits

1. Preheat the oven to 350°F. Coat a 9 x 5-inch loaf pan with cooking spray. Line the bottom and up the ends of the pan with parchment paper so it's hanging over the pan. This will make removing the bread from the pan super easy. Coat the parchment paper with the cooking spray.

2. In the bowl of a stand mixer fitted with the paddle attachment, mix the butter and sugar on medium speed for 2 minutes. Add the milk, eggs, and vanilla and continue mixing until smooth, scraping the sides of the bowl as necessary.

3. Add the mashed banana, baking powder, and salt and mix until well combined.

4. Turn the speed to low and mix in the flour until just combined. Finally, stir in the toffee bits.

5. Spread the batter in the pan and bake for 1 hour to 1 hour 5 minutes, until the center is set and a toothpick inserted in the middle comes out clean.

6. Serve warm or at room temperature.

Store airtight at room temperature for up to 3 days.

Badass Biscuits with
Salted Strawberry-Honey Butter

❖ Makes 10 biscuits ❖

*B*iscuits are one of those foods that I was late to the game in making. I went far too many years popping that blue can. Oh, the shame. Anyhow, when I pulled out my grandma's recipe and decided to put on my big-girl pants and make a scratch biscuit, life suddenly became a little brighter. Yes, I am hyperbolizing here, but honestly, a homemade biscuit on a weekend morning slathered with butter . . . well, not much is better.

And since I can't leave well enough alone, I decided to up my butter game, too. Whipping some fresh strawberries and a little honey into butter makes the freshest, tastiest biscuit topper you'll ever have. No need for jam with this butter!

. . . .

2½ cups self-rising flour
(*see DIY option*)

1 tablespoon brown sugar

½ cup (1 stick) cold salted
butter, plus 2 tablespoons
butter, melted

1 cup cold buttermilk (*DIY
option, page 25*)

All-purpose flour, for
dusting

Salted Strawberry-Honey
Butter (recipe follows)

1. Preheat the oven to 425°F. Line a baking sheet with parchment paper.

2. In a large bowl, whisk together the self-rising flour and brown sugar.

3. Using a grater, and working quickly, grate the cold butter into the flour mixture. Stir the mixture, so the flour coats the grated butter.

4. Pour the buttermilk into the bowl and stir until the mixture is combined. The dough will be sticky.

5. Transfer the dough to a lightly floured work surface. Using your hands, flatten the dough until it's 1 inch thick. Fold the dough in half and flatten it until it's 1 inch thick again. Repeat this process 4 times, flouring the surface as needed.

6. Using a biscuit cutter or a knife, cut the dough into 3-inch rounds.

7. Place the biscuits on the baking sheet and bake for 10 to 12 minutes, until golden brown.

8. As soon as the biscuits come out of the oven, brush the melted butter onto the tops and sides.

9. Serve warm or at room temperature with the strawberry butter.

Store airtight at room temperature for up to 2 days.

SALTED STRAWBERRY-HONEY BUTTER

❧ *Makes ⅔ cup* ❧

½ cup (1 stick) salted butter, at room temperature

¼ cup finely diced strawberries

1½ tablespoons honey

1 teaspoon cornstarch

Pinch of kosher salt

In the bowl of a stand mixer fitted with the paddle attachment, combine the butter, strawberries, honey, cornstarch, and salt and mix on medium speed for 3 minutes, until completely blended.

Store airtight in the refrigerator for up to 5 days.

{ DIY OPTION! }
Self-Rising Flour

❧ *Makes 4 cups* ❧

I typically use self-rising flour when I make homemade biscuits. It's an ingredient that I don't use a lot and always forget to buy at the store! The great thing is that it's simple to whip up. I make a large batch and keep it in an airtight container so I can have it when I need it.

4 cups all-purpose flour

2 tablespoons baking powder

1½ teaspoons kosher salt

In a large bowl, whisk all the ingredients together.

Store airtight for up to 6 months.

Cranberry-Orange Scones

❧ Makes 8 scones ❧

I always thought I didn't like scones. Unfortunately, based on one bad scone experience, I thought they were the driest, blandest, most confused pastry of all time. There are so many more tempting pastries out there, I had no reason to give scones a second try. But one day, in the middle of a major carb-craving, I happened upon a bakery with a VERY limited menu and decided to give the scone another shot. Desperate times, friends. Well, scones and I officially kissed and made up that day and the rest is history. A good scone for me beats out a biscuit, beats out a muffin . . . and maybe even (gasp) beats out a doughnut. I can't believe I just said that. A few years ago I started making my own scones and life has never been the same. And curiously, of all the flavors I have made from sweet to savory, these cranberry-orange scones are my most-best. Give them a try, eat them warm, and then groan at how delicious they are.

SCONES:

2 cups all-purpose flour

2 teaspoons baking powder

¼ cup granulated sugar

1 teaspoon kosher salt

4 tablespoons (½ stick) cold salted butter, cubed

1 tablespoon grated orange zest

½ cup chopped dried cranberries

¾ cup plus 4 tablespoons heavy cream

GLAZE:

1 cup powdered sugar

1 teaspoon grated orange zest

1 tablespoon orange juice

1. *For the scones:* Preheat the oven to 425°F. Line a baking sheet with parchment paper.

2. In a large bowl, whisk together the flour, baking powder, granulated sugar, and salt. Cut the butter into the mixture using a pastry cutter or a fork until the mixture resembles coarse sand. Add the orange zest and dried cranberries.

3. Make a well in the center of the dry mixture and add ¾ cup of the heavy cream. Mix the dough together. It should have a slightly dry texture, but not be crumbly. Add an additional 1 to 2 tablespoons cream if the dough seems too dry.

4. Transfer the dough to a lightly floured surface and knead it for 1 minute. Form the dough into a round 1 inch thick and use a knife or a pizza cutter to cut the round into 8 equal wedges. Arrange the wedges in a round, but about 1 inch apart, on the baking sheet. Brush the wedges with 2 tablespoons heavy cream and bake for 15 to 20 minutes, until the scones are golden and the edges are lightly toasted.

5. *For the glaze:* In a bowl, whisk together the powdered sugar, orange zest, and orange juice. Drizzle the glaze on top of the warm scones.

6. Serve the scones warm.

No-Bake Granola "Truffles"

❖ Makes 25 truffles ❖

These "truffles" are a surefire way to trick myself into thinking I'm eating healthy. While just a quick glance at the recipe list shows that this isn't exactly health food—or even breakfast food (cue evil laugh)—it is a fun alternative to a granola bar. These little bites are packed with flavor and are far more delicious than a packaged protein bar will ever be. You can make them in a snap and even adjust the ingredients to suit your own taste! It's a quick little treat that I give my kiddos for breakfast, for lunch snacks, or on the go before soccer practice!

1½ cups old-fashioned rolled oats

1 cup sweetened shredded coconut

½ cup Rice Krispies cereal

½ cup raisins

½ cup chocolate chips

½ cup peanut butter (creamy or crunchy)

¼ cup plus 1 tablespoon honey

½ teaspoon vanilla extract

¼ teaspoon kosher salt

In a large bowl, combine the oats, coconut, cereal, raisins, chocolate chips, peanut butter, honey, vanilla, and salt and stir until evenly combined. Form the mixture into 1½-inch balls, using about 2 loose tablespoons of the mixture per truffle, and pack them tightly. Transfer to a plate or container.

Store airtight at room temperature for up to 1 week.

Cookies

A balanced diet is a cookie in each hand.

There are few things better in life than a warm cookie straight out of the oven. The gooey, melty chocolate chips, the crispy edges with a slightly underbaked center—it's what cookie dreams are made of. I feel like I have a strong cookie game, referred to by me as my "Grandma Training." I plan on being not only the Gram who always has candy in her purse but also the one with warm cookies on the counter. I hope my future daughters-in-law understand this when they marry into the family. I have it all planned out: My house is for hugs and cookies. Is there any better place to be?

Soft Brown Sugar Cookies

❖ *Makes 24 cookies* ❖

*I*f you haven't noticed by now, I am a huge brown sugar fan. Honestly, I try to use it in place of granulated sugar whenever I can . . . the richness, the caramel-y flavor. I just love it. So I had to include this recipe for brown sugar cookies. One, because they are chewy and soft, and two, because they are topped with a crazy delicious brown sugar icing. These cookies are my spirit animal.

COOKIES:

¾ cup (1½ sticks) salted butter, at room temperature

1 cup packed light brown sugar

1 large egg

2 teaspoons vanilla extract

¾ teaspoon baking soda

½ teaspoon kosher salt

2 cups all-purpose flour

ICING:

4 tablespoons (½ stick) salted butter

1 cup packed light brown sugar

¼ cup heavy cream

1 teaspoon vanilla extract

1 cup powdered sugar

1. *For the cookies:* Preheat the oven to 350°F. Line a baking sheet with parchment paper.

2. In the bowl of a stand mixer fitted with the paddle attachment, mix the butter and brown sugar on medium speed for 2 minutes until the mixture is light and fluffy.

3. Add the egg and vanilla and continue mixing until smooth and combined, scraping the sides of the bowl as necessary. With the mixer still on medium, mix in the baking soda and salt until combined.

4. Turn the speed to low and add the flour, mixing only until just incorporated.

5. Using a medium (2-tablespoon) cookie scoop, drop the dough 2 inches apart on the baking sheet. Bake the cookies for 8 to 10 minutes, until the edges are lightly golden.

6. Allow the cookies to cool on the baking sheet for 2 minutes, then transfer to a wire rack to continue cooling (they can be iced when they're still warm).

7. *For the icing:* In a medium saucepan, combine the butter, brown sugar, and heavy cream and bring to a boil over medium heat, stirring frequently. Once the mixture has come to a boil, allow it to cook for 1 minute, without stirring.

8. Remove it from the heat and immediately whisk in the vanilla and powdered sugar, whisking until smooth. Allow the frosting to cool for 5 minutes and then spread onto warm or cooled cookies. (If you frost the cookies while they are still warm, the icing will melt into the cookies slightly, which is fantastic!)

Store airtight at room temperature for up to 3 days.

Light Brown Sugar

✣ *Makes 2 cups* ✣

*H*ave you ever found yourself half-way through baking a recipe, only to realize when you go to your pantry to grab the brown sugar you are out o' luck? Yep, been there, done that a time or twenty. In those moments, please don't fret. You can easily make your own in a pinch. We all have that half-full bottle of molasses sitting on our shelves that has been there since that one time we decided to make molasses cookies. Well, this is the time to use that bad boy! Homemade brown sugar is a one-way ticket to becoming a proper domestic goddess.

2 cups granulated sugar

¼ cup molasses

In a large bowl, stir together the sugar and molasses until combined and evenly light brown in color. Store airtight at room temperature for up to 6 months.

Tip: To make dark brown sugar, increase the amount of molasses to ½ cup.

S'mores Cookies

❖ Makes 24 large cookies ❖

*T*his recipe is a friends and family favorite. They are one of my most requested cookies, apart from chocolate chip. Which isn't surprising, because everyone loves s'mores, right? These cookies are packed with sweet graham cracker crumbs, bitty marshmallows, and milk chocolate, and are definitely the next best thing to sitting by a fire in the summer roasting marshmallows with your littles. I make these year-round and they are always quick to get gobbled up.

1 cup (2 sticks) salted butter, at room temperature

1½ cups packed light brown sugar

2 large eggs

2 teaspoons vanilla extract

1½ cups graham cracker crumbs

1 teaspoon baking soda

1 teaspoon kosher salt

2¼ cups all-purpose flour

1 (3-ounce) container marshmallow bits (see Tip)

2 cups coarsely chopped milk chocolate (about 6 bars) or milk chocolate chips

TOPPING:

1 cup mini marshmallows

2 milk chocolate bars broken into 24 pieces

1. Preheat the oven to 350°F. Line a baking sheet with parchment paper.

2. In the bowl of a stand mixer fitted with the paddle attachment, mix the butter and sugar on medium speed for 2 minutes until light and fluffy. Turn the speed down slightly and add the eggs and vanilla, mixing until smooth, scraping the sides of the bowl as necessary.

3. With the mixer on medium-low speed, add the graham cracker crumbs, baking soda, and salt, mixing until incorporated.

4. Turn the speed to low and beat in the flour until just combined. Stir in the marshmallow bits and chopped milk chocolate until evenly incorporated.

5. Using a large (3-tablespoon) cookie scoop, drop the dough about 2 inches apart onto the baking sheet.

6. Bake the cookies for 6 minutes, remove the pan from the oven, and press 2 or 3 mini marshmallows carefully on the tops of the cookies. Return to the oven and continue baking for 4 to 5 minutes, until the marshmallows are puffed and slightly golden and the cookie edges are lightly golden as well.

7. Remove the pan from the oven and immediately press one piece of milk chocolate onto the top of each cookie. The heat from the cookie will melt the chocolate slightly.

8. Allow the cookies to cool on the baking sheet for 2 minutes, then transfer to a wire rack to cool completely.

Store airtight at room temperature for up to 3 days.

Tip: Marshmallow bits are tiny dehydrated marshmallows. I find them at my local supermarket and the brand I use is Kraft Jet-Puffed Mallow Bits. If you can't find these, don't worry. You can easily leave them out of the cookies.

Glazed Lemmies

❧ Makes 24 cookies ❧

J am obsessed with pretty much any citrus-flavored baked good. The only downside (or upside) to this is no one else in my house likes citrus desserts. So if ever I make a lemon cookie, pie, or cake, I need to be aware that I will most likely be finishing said dessert. While not having to share sounds good in theory, in reality my jeans strongly disagree. These cookies happen to be one of my favorites, and I have been known to freeze these cookies after I make them to keep myself from eating the whole batch. Turns out these cookies are excellent frozen. I can't be saved.

COOKIES:

¾ cup (1½ sticks) salted butter, at room temperature

¾ cup granulated sugar

2 egg yolks

1 teaspoon vanilla extract

1 teaspoon grated lemon zest

1 tablespoon lemon juice

½ teaspoon kosher salt

2 cups all-purpose flour

GLAZE:

1½ cups powdered sugar

1 teaspoon grated lemon zest

2 tablespoons plus 2 teaspoons lemon juice

1. *For the cookies:* In the bowl of a stand mixer fitted with the paddle attachment, mix the butter and sugar on medium speed for 2 minutes.

2. Add the yolks, vanilla, lemon zest, lemon juice, and salt and mix for another minute until the mixture is smooth, scraping the sides of the bowl as necessary.

3. Turn the speed to low and add the flour, mixing until the dough just comes together.

4. Wrap the dough tightly in plastic wrap and chill 1 to 2 hours.

5. When you're ready to bake, preheat the oven to 350°F. Line a baking sheet with parchment paper.

6. Using a medium (2-tablespoon) cookie scoop, drop the dough 2 inches apart on the baking sheet. Bake for 10 minutes, until the edges are lightly golden.

7. Transfer the cookies to a wire rack to cool.

8. *For the glaze:* In a bowl, whisk together the powdered sugar, lemon zest, and lemon juice. Spoon or pour the glaze on top of the cookies. Allow the glaze to set before serving.

Store airtight at room temperature for up to 3 days.

Cookies and Cream Cookies

❖ Makes 30 large cookies ❖

My kids go through Oreos like every sleeve might be their last. If I have a package in the pantry and I have a batch of fresh-baked cookies on the counter, nine times out of ten they'll crack open the Oreos. And yes, my heart breaks a little bit each and every time. But I have found in life you have to work with what you've got . . . and if that means baking Oreos INTO cookies, well . . . that's what I am going to do! These cookies are ridiculously delicious, jam-packed with bits of Oreo cookie, and balanced with creamy white chocolate. Make 'em.

- -

1 cup (2 sticks) salted butter, at room temperature

1½ cups packed light brown sugar

2 large eggs

1 tablespoon vanilla extract

½ cup unsweetened cocoa powder

1 teaspoon baking soda

1 teaspoon kosher salt

2⅔ cups all-purpose flour

1 cup white chocolate chips

12 Oreo cookies, coarsely chopped

1. Preheat the oven to 350°F. Line a baking sheet with parchment paper.

2. In the bowl of a stand mixer fitted with the paddle attachment, mix the butter and brown sugar on medium speed for 2 minutes until light and fluffy.

3. Add the eggs and vanilla and continue mixing until the mixture is smooth, scraping the sides of the bowl as necessary.

4. Turn the speed to medium-low and beat in the cocoa powder, baking soda, and salt until combined and the cocoa powder is distributed evenly.

5. Turn the speed to low and add the flour, mixing until incorporated. Stir in the white chocolate chips and chopped Oreos.

6. Using a large (3-tablespoon) cookie scoop, drop the dough 2 inches apart on the baking sheet. Bake for 8 to 9 minutes, until the edges are set. Make sure not to overbake these.

7. Allow to cool on the baking sheet for 3 to 4 minutes, then transfer to a wire rack to cool completely.

Store airtight at room temperature for up to 3 days.

Coconut Macaroon Thumbprint Cookies

❧ Makes 20 cookies ❧

$\mathcal{M}$y dad happens to be a coconut macaroon expert. Not in the baking of them, but most definitely in the eating of them. I knew I wanted to include a macaroon recipe in my book and, after testing too many batches to count, I decided I liked the chewy/crunchy bits of the coconut cookie best. So this cookie is a chewy/crispy macaroon, with the perfect place in the middle to dollop a spoonful of caramel or fruit preserves. I am in LOVE with how they turned out and I know you will love them, too!

· ·

COOKIES:

3 large egg whites

½ cup granulated sugar

1 teaspoon vanilla extract

⅛ teaspoon kosher salt

14 ounces sweetened
   shredded coconut

CARAMEL TOPPING:

4 ounces soft caramels
   (such as Kraft),
   unwrapped (about 15
   pieces)

3 tablespoons heavy cream

Flaked sea salt (optional)

1. *For the cookies:* Preheat the oven to 325°F. Line a baking sheet with parchment paper or a silicone baking mat.

2. In the bowl of a stand mixer fitted with the whisk attachment, beat the egg whites, sugar, vanilla, and salt together medium-high until the mixture is foamy and the sugar is almost dissolved, 1 to 2 minutes. You don't want peaks to form.

3. Stir in the coconut.

4. Drop the coconut mixture by the heaping tablespoon onto the baking sheet. Press each mound down with the back of a spoon so they are slightly flattened with a well in the center.

5. Bake the cookies for 20 minutes, rotating the pan front to back halfway through baking.

6. *Meanwhile, make the caramel topping:* In a saucepan, combine the caramel candies and heavy cream and melt over medium-low heat, stirring frequently, until smooth.

7. When the cookies come out of the oven, spoon a teaspoon of the caramel into the centers of the cookies while they are still on the pan. Sprinkle with sea salt if desired.

8. Transfer the cookies to a wire rack to cool.

Store airtight at room temperature for up to 5 days.

Tip: If you want to fill the cookies with fruit preserves instead of caramel, follow all the steps above using 4 ounces of any flavor preserves you prefer! Or if you want to use homemade caramel, use My Favorite Caramel Sauce (page 159).

Salty Browned Butter
Chocolate Chip Cookies

❖ Makes 30 cookies ❖

*Y*es, this is another recipe for chocolate chip cookies, but I wanted to include this recipe as well as my regular go-to chocolate chip cookie (page 5), because this one is special and really different. I am a firm believer that browning butter makes most things more delicious (see my note on browning butter on page xx). Add some salt flakes to that and you have nirvana, folks. So think about a delicious gooey chocolate chip cookie made with butter that has been browned to perfection and topped off with thin flakes of sea salt. Okay, thank you. I can die now.

. . . .

1 cup (2 sticks) salted butter

2½ cups all-purpose flour

1 teaspoon baking soda

1 teaspoon coarse sea salt

1 cup packed light brown sugar

½ cup granulated sugar

2 large eggs, whisked

2 teaspoons vanilla extract

2 cups semisweet chocolate chips

Flaked sea salt, for sprinkling (optional)

1. In a medium saucepan, melt the butter over medium heat, then bring it to a boil. Once it starts boiling, swirl the pan constantly until the butter passes the foamy phase and becomes a deep amber color. Remove from the heat and allow the butter to cool for 20 minutes.

2. While the butter is cooling, preheat the oven to 350°F. Line a baking sheet with parchment paper.

3. In a large bowl, whisk together the flour, baking soda, and sea salt. Set aside.

4. Add the brown sugar, granulated sugar, eggs, and vanilla to the cooled butter in the saucepan and stir to combine. Pour this mixture into the bowl with the flour mixture. Stir using a wooden spoon until the dough comes together and the ingredients are evenly incorporated.

5. Stir in the chocolate chips.

6. Using a medium (2-tablespoon) cookie scoop, drop the dough 2 inches apart on the baking sheet. Bake for 10 to 12 minutes, until the edges are lightly golden.

7. Allow the cookies to cool for 5 minutes on the baking sheet, then transfer them to a wire rack to cool completely. If desired, sprinkle a small amount of flaked sea salt on top of the cookies as they are cooling.

Store airtight at room temperature for up to 3 days.

Crispy Chewy Oatmeal Cookies

❧ *Makes 24 large cookies* ❧

*O*atmeal cookies are like the cookie version of a tried and true friend. You know, the one who doesn't have to be the star of the show with her chocolate or sprinkles . . . the one who is always delicious even though she often gets overlooked or forgotten. She's just a constant, low-key gal pal, not in need of a ton of attention, because she's classic and confident. And when you do decide to bake her on a rainy day when you need comfort and something cozy, you're suddenly reminded why you guys are friends in the first place. Her buttery, crispy edges and her chewy, sweet center always make you smile. . . . Annnd this has officially crossed the line and gotten creepy. Just make these cookies. They are the best.

. . . .

1 cup (2 sticks) salted butter, at room temperature

1 cup packed light brown sugar

1 cup granulated sugar

2 large eggs

1 teaspoon vanilla extract

1 teaspoon kosher salt

1 teaspoon baking soda

1½ cups all-purpose flour

¾ cup sweetened flaked coconut

3 cups old-fashioned rolled oats

1 cup white chocolate chips

1. Preheat the oven to 350°F. Line a baking sheet with parchment paper.

2. In the bowl of a stand mixer fitted with the paddle attachment, mix the butter and both sugars on medium speed for 2 minutes until light and fluffy.

3. Add the eggs, vanilla, salt, and baking soda and continue mixing until smooth, scraping the sides of the bowl as necessary.

4. Turn the speed to low and add the flour, mixing until incorporated.

5. Beat in the coconut, then mix in the oats and white chocolate until evenly combined.

6. Using a large (3-tablespoon) cookie scoop, drop the dough 2 inches apart on the baking sheet.

7. Bake for 12 to 15 minutes, until the edges are golden brown and the centers have set.

8. Transfer to a wire rack to cool completely.

Store airtight at room temperature for up to 3 days.

Marbled Chocolate-Hazelnut Cookies

❖ Makes 20 large cookies ❖

*O*ne of my sons is Nutella-obsessed. If I buy a jar, I can guarantee that it will be gone by week's end. Generally we just dig in with a spoon, but I decided swirling some through a chocolate chunk cookie might be the next best thing. And it is!

2 cups plus 2 tablespoons all-purpose flour

1 tablespoon cornstarch

1 teaspoon baking soda

1 teaspoon kosher salt

¾ cup (1½ sticks) salted butter, at room temperature

¾ cup packed light brown sugar

½ cup granulated sugar

1 large egg

1 egg yolk

1 tablespoon vanilla extract

1½ cups semisweet chocolate chunks (or 12 ounces chocolate, coarsely chopped), plus an additional ½ cup for garnish (optional)

⅔ cup Nutella

1. Preheat the oven to 350°F. Line a baking sheet with parchment paper.

2. In a medium bowl, whisk together the flour, cornstarch, baking soda, and salt. Set aside.

3. In the bowl of a stand mixer fitted with the paddle attachment, beat the butter and both sugars on medium speed for 2 minutes until light and fluffy.

4. Add the whole egg, egg yolk, and vanilla and mix on medium speed for 1 minute until combined and smooth, scraping the sides of the bowl as necessary.

5. Turn the speed to low and add the flour mixture, mixing until evenly incorporated. With the mixer still on low add in 1½ cups of chocolate chunks until evenly incorporated.

6. Remove the bowl from the mixer and use a spoon to drop the Nutella by heaping spoonfuls into the cookie dough. Gently swirl the Nutella through the dough using the back end of the spoon or a butter knife. You want to see ribbons of Nutella, so be sure not to overstir.

7. Using a large (3-tablespoon) cookie scoop, drop the dough 2 inches apart on the baking sheet. Press the additional chocolate chunks on top of the cookies, if desired.

8. Bake for 9 to 10 minutes, until the edges are set.

9. Allow the cookies to cool for 3 minutes on the baking sheet, then transfer to a wire rack to cool completely.

Store airtight at room temperature for up to 3 days.

Chock-Full of White Chocolate Cookies

❖ *Makes 36 cookies* ❖

My husband is a white chocolate guy. This creamy, buttery alternative to milk or dark chocolate is his most favorite. He has a hard time turning down any white chocolate cookie, and when I created this recipe I knew he would love them. The great thing about these cookies is that people who think they don't like white chocolate try them and then promptly fall in love with this recipe! The trick is to use good-quality white chocolate and chop it up into medium-size chunks. When they are baked up and eaten warm, the white chocolate is soft and gooey!

. . . .

1 cup (2 sticks) salted butter, at room temperature

1 cup packed light brown sugar

½ cup granulated sugar

2 large eggs

1½ tablespoons vanilla extract

1 teaspoon kosher salt

1 teaspoon baking soda

½ teaspoon baking powder

2½ cups all-purpose flour

20 ounces white chocolate, coarsely chopped (or 2½ to 3 cups white chocolate chips)

1. Preheat the oven to 350°F. Line a baking sheet with parchment paper.

2. In the bowl of a stand mixer fitted with the paddle attachment, mix together the butter and both sugars on medium speed for 2 minutes.

3. Add the eggs and vanilla and mix until smooth, scraping the sides of the bowl as necessary.

4. Turn the mixer speed to low and add the salt, baking soda, baking powder, and flour, mixing until just combined.

5. Stir in the white chocolate chunks or white chocolate chips.

6. Using a medium (2-tablespoon) cookie scoop, drop the dough 2 inches apart on the baking sheet.

7. Bake for 8 to 10 minutes, until golden around the edges. Don't overbake.

8. Allow the cookies to cool on the baking sheet for 3 to 5 minutes, then transfer to a wire rack to cool completely.

Store airtight at room temperature for up to 3 days.

Flourless Chocolate Cookies
with Flaked Sea Salt

⸙ Makes 20 cookies ⸙

*T*hese cookies are chewy and totally chocolaty. There is actually no butter involved and only egg whites are used . . . so basically, what I am saying is that this might as well be the dessert equivalent of a kale smoothie. Okay, not really, I'm kidding! But they are lighter in calories and fat while being insanely jam-packed with flavor. Oh, and you don't need a mixer on this one either, just a bowl and a whisk! The chocolate shines in a huge way, and adding the flaked sea salt on top makes everything come together perfectly.

2½ cups powdered sugar

⅔ cup unsweetened cocoa powder

2 teaspoons cornstarch

½ teaspoon kosher salt

3 large egg whites, lightly beaten

⅔ cup mini semisweet chocolate chips

2 tablespoons flaked sea salt

1. Preheat the oven to 350°F. Line a baking sheet with parchment paper and coat lightly with cooking spray.

2. In a bowl, whisk together the powdered sugar, cocoa powder, cornstarch, and salt. Mix in the egg whites until smooth. Stir in the chocolate chips.

3. Drop the dough by the tablespoon, 2 inches apart, onto the baking sheet.

4. Bake for 12 to 15 minutes, until the tops are set and crackly.

5. Sprinkle the cookies with sea salt immediately when they come out of the oven.

6. Transfer the cookies to a wire rack to cool completely.

Store airtight at room temperature for up to 2 days.

Key Lime Pie Cookies

❖ Makes 36 cookies ❖

*K*ey lime pie is one of my favorite desserts. The creamy, cool, smooth texture paired with the crunchy graham cracker crust just gets me every time. I knew I wanted to create a cookie with all the same qualities of my favorite pie, but omitting the creamy filling and getting all the flavor packed into a cookie was tricky. Fortunately I was able to perform some cookie sorcery and, with a few pulses of the mixer, a bright and cheery cookie was born.

1 cup (2 sticks) salted
butter, at room
temperature

1¼ cups granulated sugar

1 large egg

1 teaspoon vanilla extract

3 tablespoons Key lime
juice

2 teaspoons grated lime
zest

½ teaspoon kosher salt

½ teaspoon baking soda

2¼ cups all-purpose flour

1 cup finely crushed
graham cracker crumbs

½ cup white chocolate

1. Preheat the oven to 350°F. Line a baking sheet with parchment paper.

2. In the bowl of a stand mixer fitted with the paddle attachment, mix the butter and sugar on medium speed for 2 minutes until light and fluffy.

3. Add the egg, vanilla, key lime juice, and lime zest and continue mixing for 1 more minute, scraping the sides of the bowl as necessary. Mix in the salt and baking soda until incorporated.

4. Turn the speed to low and add the flour and graham cracker crumbs until the dough comes together.

5. Roll the dough into 1-inch balls and place 2 inches apart on the baking sheet. Bake for 9 to 10 minutes, until the edges are lightly golden.

6. Transfer the cookies to a wire rack to cool.

7. Place the white chocolate in a microwave-safe bowl. Heat on full power for 25 seconds. Remove the bowl from the microwave and stir the chocolate. Repeat this process until the white chocolate is melted and smooth. Transfer the melted chocolate to a small zip-top bag. Snip one corner of the bag off with scissors and drizzle the white chocolate on top of the cookies. Allow the white chocolate to set completely.

Store the cookies airtight at room temperature for up to 3 days.

Pound Cake Cookies

❧ Makes 24 cookies ❧

These cookies are a little something for those of you who like cakey cookies. These buttery morsels of goodness somehow manage to be both dense and fluffy at the same time. Of course I like to heap frosting on top of them, but they are also great with just a light dusting of powdered sugar. These cookies are simple, tasty, and classic.

2¼ cups all-purpose flour

½ teaspoon kosher salt

½ teaspoon baking powder

½ cup (1 stick) salted butter, at room temperature

¾ cup granulated sugar

1 large egg

1 egg yolk

1½ teaspoons vanilla extract

½ cup whole milk

Powdered sugar, for dusting (optional)

1. Preheat the oven to 350°F. Line a baking sheet with parchment paper.

2. In a large bowl, whisk together the flour, salt, and baking powder. Set aside.

3. In the bowl of a stand mixer fitted with the paddle attachment, beat the butter and sugar on medium speed for 2 minutes. Add the whole egg, egg yolk, and vanilla and continue mixing until combined, scraping the sides of the bowl as necessary.

4. Turn the speed to low and add one-third of the flour mixture and half of the milk, beating well after each addition. Repeat this step. End with a final addition of the flour mixture. Mix until combined and smooth, scraping the sides of the bowl as necessary.

5. Using a medium (2-tablespoon) cookie scoop, drop the dough 2 inches apart on the baking sheet.

6. Bake for 10 minutes, until set and lightly golden at the edges, rotating the baking sheet front to back once during baking.

7. Transfer the cookies to a wire rack to cool completely.

8. If desired, dust the cookies with powdered sugar.

Store the cookies airtight at room temperature for up to 2 days.

Tip: I also recommend frosting the cookies with Glaze Icing (page 171).

Peanut Butter Cup–Filled Brownie Cookie Sandwiches

*S*eeing as how peanut butter cups were really the inspiration for the "cups" in the Cookies and Cups name (see page xii for more on this), I knew I had to feature them in my book. And these brownie-cookie sandwiches are the perfect vehicle for the peanut butter cups. The cookies are chewy and chocolaty, and when a peanut butter cup is placed between them when they're warm, they all live happily ever after in an outrageous cookie love-sandwich.

½ cup (1 stick) salted butter

1 pound semisweet chocolate, chopped

1 cup all-purpose flour

1 teaspoon baking powder

½ teaspoon kosher salt

4 large eggs

1½ cups packed light brown sugar

2 teaspoons vanilla extract

12 regular-size peanut butter cups

1. Preheat the oven to 350°F. Line a baking sheet with parchment paper.

2. In a medium saucepan, melt the butter and chocolate over low heat, stirring frequently until the ingredients are just melted. Remove the pan from the heat and allow the butter-chocolate mixture to cool for 5 minutes.

3. Meanwhile, in a medium bowl, whisk together the flour, baking powder, and salt. Set aside.

4. In a large bowl, whisk together the eggs, brown sugar, and vanilla. Add the butter-chocolate mixture to the egg mixture slowly, stirring as you go. Stir in the flour mixture until combined.

5. Scoop the dough by the heaping tablespoon and place on the baking sheet 2 inches apart. Bake for 9 to 10 minutes until the cookies are set in the middle.

6. Allow the cookies to cool on the baking sheet for 3 minutes. Then flip half of the cookies over carefully and place a peanut butter cup on each flipped cookie. Place the remaining cookies on top of the peanut butter cups while they are warm. The heat of the cookies will gradually melt the peanut butter cups enough to hold the sandwiches together.

7. Allow the cookie sandwiches to cool completely on a wire rack.

Store airtight at room temperature for up to 3 days.

Sparkling Apple Cider Meltaway Cookies

❖ Makes 24 cookies ❖

*M*eltaway cookies are a hidden treasure. The smooth texture that you get from adding cornstarch to the dough is pretty great. Pairing that texture with the nuttiness of browned butter and the brightness of sparkling apple cider makes these cookies simple perfection. There are a few steps to this cookie, but I promise it's all worth it in the end!

COOKIES:

1 cup (2 sticks) salted butter

1½ cups all-purpose flour

½ cup powdered sugar

½ cup cornstarch

½ teaspoon kosher salt

2 tablespoons sparkling apple cider

GLAZE:

1¼ cups powdered sugar

2 tablespoons sparkling apple cider

1. *For the cookies:* In a medium saucepan, melt the butter over medium heat, then bring it to a boil. Once it starts boiling, swirl the pan constantly until the butter passes the foamy phase and becomes a deep amber color. Remove from the heat and chill it for at least 1 hour in the refrigerator until it becomes a solid. You can chill the butter directly in the pan or transfer it to a smaller container to chill.

2. Next, remove the butter from the refrigerator and allow it to come back up to room temperature.

3. In a medium bowl, whisk together the flour, sugar, cornstarch, and salt. Set aside.

4. In the bowl of a stand mixer fitted with the paddle attachment, beat the browned butter on medium speed until smooth.

5. Turn the speed to low and slowly add the flour mixture, mixing until the dough comes together. Add the apple cider and mix until combined.

6. Divide the dough in half and roll each half into a log 8 to 9 inches long. Wrap the logs separately in plastic wrap and chill for 2 to 3 hours.

7. When you're ready to bake, preheat the oven to 350°F. Line a baking sheet with parchment paper.

8. Remove the dough from the refrigerator and unwrap the logs. Slice the logs crosswise into ½-inch-thick rounds. Place the cookies on the baking sheet. Bake for 9 to 10 minutes, until the edges are lightly golden.

9. Transfer the cookies to a wire rack to cool completely.

10. *For the glaze:* In a medium bowl, whisk together the powdered sugar and apple cider until smooth. Spoon or pour the glaze on the top of each cookie. Allow the glaze to set before serving.

Store the cookies airtight at room temperature for up to 5 days.

Brownies and Bars

My happiness resides in a 9 x 13 pan.

B rownies and their dreamboat second cousin, the cookie bar, are my true loves. They are the heart of my website and one of my favorite things to bake. (I know what you're thinking—but www.brownies andcookiebarsandcups.com just didn't have the same ring to it, okay?!) I love the ease of a one-pan dessert . . . I mean cookies are great, we all love cookies, but you have to scoop and bake and scoop and bake. And cakes, bless their hearts, are gorgeous and special, but they are finicky and tedious with all their steps and frosting. But bar desserts—they're my homies, both laid-back and sexy at the same time. You can eat them out of the pan, or serve them up to guests. No rules, no judgment.

Kitchen Sink Blondies

❖ Makes 30 bars ❖

*T*hese bars pretty much sum up my favorite dessert style. They're indulgent, a little excessive, salty/sweet, and kinda trashy. They are brown sugar blondies, loaded with chopped Oreo cookies, chopped Snickers bars, Heath bar bits, chocolate chips, caramel sauce, and kettle chips. Yes, pretty much everything but the kitchen sink *nudge nudge, wink wink.* My website is founded on over-the-top sweets, which are these bars in a nutshell. But, with all that said, they somehow aren't *too* sweet. They are chewy and rich, but the thick-cut kettle chips balance everything out nicely.

- 3 cups kettle-style potato chips
- 1 cup (2 sticks) salted butter, at room temperature
- 1¼ cups packed light brown sugar
- 2 large eggs
- 1 tablespoon vanilla extract
- 1 teaspoon baking soda
- 1 teaspoon kosher salt
- 2½ cups all-purpose flour
- 4 (1.86-ounce) Snickers bars, coarsely chopped
- 10 Oreo cookies, coarsely chopped
- ½ cup Heath Milk Chocolate Toffee Bits
- 1 cup semisweet chocolate chips
- ¼ cup caramel sauce, homemade (page 159) or store-bought

1. Preheat the oven to 350°F. Line a 9 x 13-inch baking dish with foil and coat liberally with cooking spray.

2. Spread the kettle chips evenly in the bottom of the coated pan and set aside.

3. In the bowl of a stand mixer fitted with the paddle attachment, mix the butter and brown sugar on medium speed for 2 minutes.

4. Add the eggs, vanilla, baking soda, and salt and continue mixing until smooth, scraping the sides of the bowl as necessary.

5. Turn the speed to low and add the flour, mixing until incorporated.

6. Turn the mixer off and add three-fourths of the chopped Snickers, the chopped Oreos, toffee bits, and chocolate chips to the bowl. Stir by hand using a wooden spoon or rubber spatula until combined evenly. Do not overmix.

7. Carefully press the mixture evenly into the pan over the layer of potato chips. Try your best not to crush the chips completely.

8. Sprinkle with the remaining chopped Snickers and press the pieces into the top of the dough. Drizzle the caramel sauce evenly over everything.

9. Bake for 20 to 25 minutes, until the edges are set. The middle might seem slightly undercooked, this is okay.

10. Allow the bars to cool completely before cutting.

Store airtight at room temperature for up to 3 days.

Tip: Serve these with ice cream and caramel sauce for a truly indulgent dessert!

Strawberries and Cream Bars

✢ Makes 16 bars ✢

*F*ull disclosure: I have never been a huge fan of fruit in desserts. I mean, I like it fine, but if I had the choice between a peanut butter cup or a fruit tart . . . well . . . sorry, fruits, you lose. Apparently, though, there is a whole big, bad world out there that loves fruit as much as I love chocolate. Who knew?

In order to appeal to the masses, I created these strawberries and cream bars that I ended up loving as much as I love a s'more. I am officially a changed woman.

. . . .

BARS:

1 cup (2 sticks) salted butter, at room temperature

1 cup granulated sugar

1 teaspoon vanilla extract

2 cups all-purpose flour

TOPPING:

8 ounces cream cheese, at room temperature

1 cup white chocolate chips, melted

1½ cups chopped strawberries

1. *For the bars:* Preheat the oven to 350°F. Line a 7 x 11-inch baking dish with foil and coat lightly with cooking spray.

2. In the bowl of a stand mixer fitted with the paddle attachment, mix the butter, sugar, and vanilla on medium speed for 2 minutes.

3. Turn the speed to low and add the flour, mixing until the dough just comes together.

4. Press the dough into the prepared pan and bake for 30 minutes, or until the edges are golden.

5. Remove the pan from the oven and allow to cool completely.

6. *For the topping:* In the bowl of a stand mixer fitted with the paddle attachment, beat the cream cheese on medium speed until smooth. Slowly beat in the melted white chocolate and mix on medium speed until smooth and incorporated evenly, scraping the sides of the bowl as necessary.

7. Spread the cream cheese mixture on top of the cooled crust. Place the pan in the refrigerator to chill for at least 30 minutes.

8. When you're ready to serve the bars, spread the strawberries evenly on top of the cream cheese layer.

Store airtight in the refrigerator for up to 2 days.

Tuxedo Brownies

❖ Makes 30 bars ❖

*N*ow here is a knock-your-socks-off, over-the-top, super-rich-and-decadent brownie. Interested? I thought so. The dark, fudgy brownie paired with the creamy, buttery frosting topped with a rich chocolate ganache is SURE to please the chocolate lover in your life. If you haven't picked up on this yet, I don't really buy into the expression "less is more," especially when it comes to desserts, and this bar is a prime example of excess done right.

BROWNIES:

2 cups semisweet chocolate chips

½ cup (1 stick) salted butter

¾ cup packed light brown sugar

¾ cup granulated sugar

4 large eggs

2 teaspoons vanilla extract

½ teaspoon kosher salt

1 cup all-purpose flour

FROSTING LAYER:

½ cup (1 stick) butter, at room temperature

3 cups powdered sugar

2 tablespoons heavy cream

GANACHE TOPPING:

1 cup semisweet chocolate chips

½ cup heavy cream

1. *For the brownies:* Preheat the oven to 325°F. Line a 9 x 13-inch baking dish with foil and coat with cooking spray.

2. In a medium saucepan, combine the chocolate chips and butter and melt over medium-low heat, stirring frequently. Remove from the heat as soon as the chocolate is melted.

3. Whisk both sugars into the melted chocolate. Add the eggs, vanilla, and salt and whisk to combine. Stir in the flour until evenly mixed in.

4. Pour into the prepared pan and bake for 35 to 40 minutes, until a toothpick inserted 2 inches from the edge of the pan comes out clean. The center may seem underbaked slightly, but this is fine.

5. Allow the brownies to cool completely in the pan.

6. *For the frosting layer:* When you are ready to assemble the brownies, in the bowl of a stand mixer fitted with the paddle attachment, mix the butter, powdered sugar, and cream on medium speed until creamy. Spread this evenly onto the cooled brownies. Place the pan in the refrigerator to chill while you prepare the ganache topping.

7. *For the ganache topping:* Place the chocolate chips in a heatproof bowl.

8. In a small saucepan, heat the cream over medium heat until it starts steaming and is almost boiling. Immediately remove from the heat and pour over the chocolate chips. Stir the cream and the chocolate together until the mixture is smooth. Allow the ganache to cool for 5 minutes.

9. Remove the brownies from the refrigerator and spread the ganache evenly onto the frosting layer. Return the pan back to the refrigerator for 30 minutes until the chocolate is set.

10. Cut into bars and serve.

Store airtight at room temperature for up to 3 days.

Gooey Salted Caramel Chocolate Chip Cookie Bars

❧ Makes 30 bars ❧

*I*f you haven't already detected a pattern in this book, I am a bit of a salted caramel fanatic. Whenever I can add a bit of flaked sea salt on top of a caramel-tinged dessert to really draw out the flavor, I'll do it. No shame in my game. These bars are every bit as delicious as you would imagine them to be. They're super gooey and loaded with chocolate, with a creamy caramel center. Of course a little goes a long way, so these are perfect for a party!

1 cup (2 sticks) salted butter, at room temperature

1 cup packed light brown sugar

½ cup granulated sugar

2 large eggs

1 teaspoon vanilla extract

1 teaspoon kosher salt

1 teaspoon baking soda

2½ cups all-purpose flour

2 cups semisweet chocolate chips

1 (14-ounce) can sweetened condensed milk

10 ounces soft caramels (such as Kraft), unwrapped (about 40 pieces)

1 teaspoon flaked sea salt

1. Preheat the oven to 350°F. Line a 9 x 13-inch baking dish with foil and coat liberally with cooking spray.

2. In the bowl of a stand mixer fitted with the paddle attachment, mix the butter and both sugars on medium speed for 2 minutes until fluffy.

3. Add the eggs, vanilla, salt, and baking soda and continue mixing until smooth, scraping the sides of the bowl as necessary.

4. Turn the speed to low and add the flour until combined. Stir in the chocolate chips.

5. Press half of the dough into the prepared pan.

6. In a medium saucepan, combine the condensed milk and caramels and cook over medium-low heat, stirring frequently, until the caramels are melted.

7. Pour the caramel mixture on top of the dough in the pan and drop the remaining dough evenly in teaspoon-size amounts on top of the caramel.

8. Bake for 25 to 30 minutes, until the center is just set.

9. Sprinkle with flaked sea salt.

10. Allow to cool completely in the pan before cutting into bars.

Store airtight at room temperature for up to 3 days.

Blueberry Cobbler Cheesecake Bars
with a Macadamia Nut Crust

❖ Makes 30 bars ❖

*T*his recipe is just an all-around solid winner. First off, it's cheesecake you can eat with your hands. If that alone doesn't sell you, you might need to check your pulse. Second, it has a streusel topping, which makes just about any dish more delicious. And finally, it has a crust made with macadamia nuts and coconut. Even my friend who claims she "doesn't like coconut" went back for seconds on these. So really what I am saying is you need to run to the store and grab up the ingredients to make these. You can thank me later.

. . . .

CRUST:

½ cup (1 stick) salted butter, melted

1 cup graham cracker crumbs

½ cup all-purpose flour

½ cup sweetened flaked coconut

½ cup finely chopped macadamia nuts

¼ cup granulated sugar

CHEESECAKE LAYER:

12 ounces cream cheese, at room temperature

⅔ cup granulated sugar

4 large eggs

1 teaspoon vanilla extract

2 cups fresh blueberries, or frozen and thawed

STREUSEL TOPPING:

1 cup packed light brown sugar

¾ cup all-purpose flour

7 tablespoons cold salted butter, cubed

1. *For the crust:* Preheat the oven to 350°F. Line a 9 x 13-inch baking dish with foil and coat with cooking spray.

2. In a large bowl, mix together the melted butter, graham cracker crumbs, flour, coconut, nuts, and granulated sugar. Press the mixture evenly into the bottom of the prepared pan.

3. Bake the crust for 8 to 10 minutes, until lightly golden. Remove from the oven, but leave the oven on.

4. *For the cheesecake layer:* In the bowl of a stand mixer fitted with the paddle attachment, mix the cream cheese and sugar on medium speed until smooth, scraping the sides of the bowl as necessary. Add the eggs, one at a time, mixing until smooth after each addition. Add the vanilla and mix until well incorporated.

5. Stir in the blueberries carefully and pour the mixture over the warm crust.

6. *For the streusel topping:* In a medium bowl, combine the brown sugar, flour, and butter and mix with a pastry cutter or your hands, forming the mixture into large crumbs.

7. Sprinkle the streusel topping over the cream cheese filling and return the pan to the oven. Bake for 20 to 25 minutes, until the center is set.

8. Cool the bars in the pan on a wire rack for 30 minutes and then cover and place in the refrigerator for at least 2 hours to chill completely.

9. Cut into bars when you're ready to serve.

Store airtight in the refrigerator for up to 3 days.

Confetti White Chocolate Bars

❧ *Makes 16 bars* ❧

*T*hese buttery and rich bars are a total party! We all know life is better covered in sprinkles, so when I get a chance to add a little extra happy into a recipe I jump on it! These cookie bars are really easy, and even if white chocolate's not your thing, you could switch them up and use milk or semisweet chocolate chips instead. The trick to making them extra pretty is to use quin sprinkles (also known as confetti sprinkles) or jimmies sprinkles (also known as ice cream sprinkles). Nonpareil sprinkles, while adorable, will leak color all over your batter and make it . . . well . . . not as cute. So hurry and make these soft and chewy bars, and you have my permission to get crazy and go heavy-handed with the sprinkles!

½ cup (1 stick) salted butter, at room temperature

¾ cup packed light brown sugar

1 large egg

2 teaspoons vanilla extract

1 teaspoon baking powder

½ teaspoon kosher salt

1¼ cups all-purpose flour

1½ cups white chocolate chips

½ cup rainbow sprinkles, plus 2 tablespoons for garnish

1. Preheat the oven to 350°F. Line an 8 x 8-inch baking dish with foil and coat with cooking spray.

2. In the bowl of a stand mixer fitted with the paddle attachment, mix the butter and brown sugar on medium speed for 2 minutes. Add the egg, vanilla, baking powder, and salt and continue mixing for 1 minute, scraping the sides of the bowl as necessary.

3. Turn the speed to low and add the flour, mixing until just combined. Stir in the white chocolate chips and ½ cup sprinkles until evenly incorporated.

4. Press the dough into the prepared pan, top with the additional 2 tablespoons of sprinkles, and bake for 20 to 25 minutes, until the edges are lightly golden brown.

5. Allow to cool in the pan on a wire rack.

6. Cut into bars when you're ready to serve.

Store airtight at room temperature for up to 3 days.

Junk Food Marshmallow Squares

*D*on't be scared by the name of these ooey, gooey, salty, sweet bars. I am a marshmallow square fanatic with the firm belief that anything coated in a healthy dose of melted marshmallows will be delicious. It might seem crazy to coat salty snacks in sweet mallows, but the result is nothing short of perfection. Play around with the add-ins if you want, but I have found the combo of chips, pretzels, and popcorn is stellar. Oh, did I mention there is browned butter mixed into the whole mess? Yeah . . . that.

. . . .

4 tablespoons (½ stick) salted butter

8 cups mini marshmallows

2 cups coarsely crushed wavy potato chips

2 cups coarsely crushed pretzels

1 cup popped buttered popcorn (microwave or prepared store-bought)

1. Line a 9 x 9-inch baking dish with foil and coat lightly with cooking spray.

2. In a large saucepan, melt the butter over medium heat, then bring it to a boil. Once it starts boiling, swirl the pan constantly until the butter passes the foamy phase and becomes a deep amber color. Immediately add the marshmallows and continue stirring until the marshmallows are melted. Remove the pan from the heat.

3. Quickly stir in the potato chips, pretzels, and popcorn and make sure to coat them in the melted marshmallows.

4. Transfer the mixture immediately to the prepared dish, pressing it evenly but without packing the mixture too tightly.

5. Allow the mixture to cool and then cut into squares.

Best if served the same day, but you can store airtight at room temperature for up to 2 days if necessary.

Salted Caramel Apple Butter Bars

❖ Makes 28 bars ❖

A version of these bars is on my website and it has consistently been one of the most popular recipes on my site, for as long as I have been blogging. And for good reason: These bars are phenomenal. I knew I wanted to include them in my book, but I wanted to change the recipe up a bit. I knew the addition of sliced apples would send these to a whole new level. The mild sweetness of the apples paired with the salty sweetness of the caramel makes every bite a whole experience. Please don't be scared of the amount of butter in these little gems. A little goes a long way, indeed.

- 2 cups (1 pound) salted butter, at room temperature
- 2 cups granulated sugar
- 1 tablespoon vanilla extract
- 4 cups all-purpose flour
- 14 ounces soft caramels (such as Kraft), unwrapped (about 55 pieces)
- ⅓ cup heavy cream
- 1 tablespoon flaked sea salt
- 2 large Granny Smith apples, peeled and thinly sliced

1. Preheat the oven to 325°F. Line a 9 x 13-inch baking dish with foil and coat lightly with cooking spray.

2. In the bowl of a stand mixer fitted with the paddle attachment, mix the butter and sugar on medium speed for 2 minutes, until light and fluffy.

3. Add the vanilla and continue mixing until incorporated.

4. Turn the speed to low and slowly add the flour until the dough comes together.

5. Divide the dough in half. Press half into the bottom of the prepared pan. Wrap the other half in plastic wrap and refrigerate until needed.

6. Bake the base for 15 to 20 minutes, until the edges begin to turn golden brown. Transfer the pan to a wire rack to cool slightly, but leave the oven on while you do the next steps.

7. In a medium saucepan, combine the caramels and cream and melt over medium-low heat, stirring frequently. Once the caramel is melted and smooth, pour this evenly on top of the baked base.

8. Sprinkle the sea salt evenly onto the caramel and layer the apples on the caramel evenly, overlapping where necessary.

9. Remove the reserved dough from the refrigerator and crumble it evenly on top of the apples.

10. Bake for 30 to 35 minutes, until the top is lightly golden brown and the caramel is bubbling.

11. Allow to cool completely before cutting into bars.

Store airtight at room temperature for up to 2 days.

No-Bake Mint Chocolate Bars

❧ Makes 25 bars ❧

*O*ne of my kiddos is obsessed with all things mint/chocolate. It seems to be a flavor that some people really love, and I have to say that, while it's no salted caramel in my book, I am pretty fond of it myself. These bars are outrageously good. They're both crunchy and creamy, cool and rich. And they happen to be a no-bake recipe, which makes them a cinch to whip up for any occasion!

CRUST:

25 Oreo cookies, crushed

⅓ cup finely chopped chocolate mint candies (such as Andes)

MINT LAYER:

4 tablespoons (½ stick) salted butter, at room temperature

2 cups powdered sugar

½ teaspoon peppermint extract

1 tablespoon heavy cream

1 to 2 drops green food coloring

TOPPING:

1¼ cups chopped chocolate mint candies (such as Andes)

¼ cup heavy cream

1. *For the crust:* Line a 9 x 9-inch baking dish with foil and coat the foil lightly with cooking spray.

2. Place the crushed Oreos in a large bowl. Set aside.

3. In a medium microwave-safe bowl, microwave the chocolate mint candies in 30-second intervals, stirring after each interval, until the candies are fully melted.

4. Pour the melted candies into the Oreo crumbs and stir to coat evenly. Press the mixture into the prepared baking dish using the bottom of a glass or the back of a spoon to pack it down firmly. Place the crust in the refrigerator while you prepare the mint layer.

5. *For the mint layer:* In the bowl of a stand mixer fitted with the paddle attachment, beat the butter on medium speed for 1 minute until smooth. Turn the speed to low and beat the powdered sugar into the butter until combined. Add the peppermint extract, cream, and food coloring, turn the speed back up to medium, and beat until smooth and creamy.

6. Remove the crust from the refrigerator and evenly spread the filling on top. Return to the refrigerator while you prepare the topping.

7. *For the topping:* In a medium microwave-safe bowl, microwave the chopped candies and heavy cream in 30-second intervals, stirring after each interval, until the candies are melted and the mixture is smooth.

8. Remove the baking dish from the refrigerator and pour the melted chocolate mixture on top, spreading it evenly over the filling.

9. Return the dish to the refrigerator for at least 30 minutes until the top is set.

10. Cut into bars when ready to serve.

Store airtight in the refrigerator for up to 3 days.

I n...
weak...
servi...
I say...

. . . .

BARS:

1 cup
    butte
    temp

1 cup
    suga

1 egg

1 teasp

½ teas

2 cups

FROST

5 table

1 cup
    suga

¼ cup

1 cup

½ cup

Tip:
warm.
ing it o

Birthday Cake Krispie Treats

❖ Makes 24 bars ❖

There is really no better sweet treat than this one right here. It has all the makings of a classic—because it's two classics mashed together! This recipe is a spin on a popular one on my website, the Red Velvet Krispie Treats, which also happen to be a pretty genius idea courtesy of my youngest kiddo. My whole family likes to get involved in recipe development and the simple idea of adding dry cake mix to Rice Krispie Treats produces pretty stellar results! These would be so perfect for any party as an alternative to cake.

KRISPIES:

4 tablespoons (½ stick) salted butter

10 ounces mini marshmallows

⅓ cup dry confetti cake mix

6 cups Rice Krispies cereal

¼ cup rainbow sprinkles

FILLING:

½ cup (1 stick) salted butter, at room temperature

2 cups powdered sugar

1 tablespoon heavy cream

1. *For the krispies:* Line an 11 x 17-inch rimmed baking sheet with foil and coat lightly with cooking spray.

2. In a large pot, melt the butter over medium-low heat. As soon as it's melted, add the marshmallows and stir until they are just melted. Immediately remove the pot from the heat and stir in the dry cake mix to combine with the marshmallows. Add in the Rice Krispies and the sprinkles, stirring to incorporate them completely with the marshmallow mixture.

3. Press the mixture evenly into the prepared pan. Set it aside to cool.

4. *For the filling:* In the bowl of a stand mixer fitted with the paddle attachment, beat the butter on medium speed until smooth. Turn the speed to low and slowly add the powdered sugar and cream. Gradually turn the mixer speed back up to medium and beat the frosting for 1 minute until creamy, scraping the sides of the bowl as necessary.

5. When the krispie layer has cooled, cut it crosswise in half. Coat one-half of the krispies with the frosting, leaving a ½-inch border around the edges. Place the other half on top of the frosting to create a giant sandwich, pressing down lightly.

6. Cut the krispie treats into bars when you are ready to serve them.

Store airtight at room temperature for up to 3 days.

Tip: Use a piece of parchment or wax paper coated lightly with cooking spray to help press the mixture into the pan to avoid sticky bits all over your fingers!

Creamy Coconut-Lime Squares

❖ Makes 16 squares ❖

*O*ne of my favorite flavor combinations is coconut and lime. I feel like the tartness of the lime balances perfectly with the creaminess of the coconut. And these aren't just any lime squares . . . the rich lime filling sits on top of a coconut shortbread made extra delicious with the use of coconut oil and coconut flakes. You could easily eat the crust on its own, cutting it into cute little shortbread wedges, but you should really top it with the cool, creamy lime. It's just the right thing to do.

. . . .

CRUST:

½ cup plus 2 tablespoons coconut oil (in the solid state)

¼ teaspoon kosher salt

⅓ cup powdered sugar

½ cup sweetened flaked coconut

1¼ cups all-purpose flour

LIME FILLING:

3 egg yolks

1 (14-ounce) can sweetened condensed milk

1 tablespoon grated lime zest

½ cup lime juice

1. *For the crust:* Preheat the oven to 350°F. Line an 8 x 8-inch pan with foil and coat lightly with cooking spray.

2. In the bowl of a stand mixer fitted with the paddle attachment, beat the coconut oil, salt, and powdered sugar together on medium speed until smooth. Add the flaked coconut and flour and continue mixing until incorporated. The mixture will be crumbly, but it will hold together when squeezed.

3. Press the dough evenly into the pan. Bake the crust for 15 to 20 minutes, until the edges are lightly golden. (When the crust is done, leave the oven on.)

4. *Meanwhile, for the lime filling:* In the clean bowl of a stand mixer fitted with the whisk attachment, mix the egg yolks on medium speed for 2 minutes. Add the condensed milk and mix on medium speed for 2 minutes. Add the lime zest and lime juice and mix on medium speed for 2 more minutes.

5. Pour the lime filling onto the warm, baked crust. Return to the oven and bake for 10 to 15 minutes, until the lime layer is just set. Let cool in the pan for 20 minutes, then transfer the pan to the refrigerator to cool completely, at least 2 hours.

6. When chilled, cut into squares and serve.

Store airtight in the refrigerator for up to 3 days.

Chocolate-Hazelnut Brownies

❧ Makes 12 brownies ❧

J remember the first time I tried Nutella spread. I was 24 years old and I had just moved to New Jersey from Texas. My husband (then boyfriend) bought a jar at the supermarket and left it out on the counter. I walked over and picked up the jar, wondering why in the world I would want chocolate-hazelnut spread in my life. Well, after that first bite the rest was history, and Nutella has gone on to become my main squeeze. It's true, I adore it. Mixing Nutella into brownies seems like the obvious choice and I will tell you—no bias, of course—my recipe is stellar. You won't find a better brownie!

⅓ cup salted butter, at room temperature

½ cup packed light brown sugar

2 large eggs

2 teaspoons vanilla extract

1¼ cups Nutella, divided

½ teaspoon kosher salt

¾ cup all-purpose flour

1. Preheat the oven to 350°F. Line an 8 x 8-inch baking dish with foil and coat with cooking spray.

2. In the bowl of a stand mixer fitted with the paddle attachment, mix the butter and brown sugar on medium speed for 2 minutes. With the mixer still on medium, add the eggs and vanilla and continue mixing until smooth, scraping the sides of the bowl as necessary.

3. Turn the speed to medium-low and add 1 cup of the Nutella and the salt, mixing until smooth and fluffy.

4. Turn the speed to low and add the flour, mixing until just combined.

5. Spread the batter evenly into the prepared pan. Drop the remaining ¼ cup Nutella by the teaspoon evenly over the batter, then swirl the Nutella into the batter using a butter knife.

6. Bake for 30 to 35 minutes, until the center is just set.

7. Allow to cool completely in the pan on a wire rack. Cut into squares when ready to serve.

Store airtight at room temperature for up to 3 days.

No-Bake Chocolate-Filled Oat Squares

Makes 16 squares

I love a no-bake bar, and these can be whipped up in minutes and snacked on throughout the week! My kids love these treats in their lunchboxes or as an afternoon snack. They're a fun spin on a granola bar, but also slightly richer and more decadent. For this recipe, unlike most of my others, I use unsalted butter, or sometimes even substitute coconut oil for the butter in equal amounts. There is a lot of room for creativity with these easy bars!

¾ cup (1½ sticks) unsalted butter or coconut oil (measured in its solid state)

½ cup packed light brown sugar

2½ cups quick-cooking oats

⅓ cup creamy peanut butter

¾ cup semisweet chocolate chips

1. Line an 8 x 8-inch pan with foil and set aside.

2. In a medium saucepan, combine the butter and brown sugar and bring to a boil over medium heat. Boil for 2 minutes, then remove the pan from the heat and stir in the oats. Set the pan aside to cool slightly while you melt the peanut butter and chocolate.

3. In the top of a double boiler, combine the peanut butter and chocolate chips. Melt them together, stirring constantly over simmering water. When the chocolate is melted and smooth, set the mixture aside.

4. Press half of the oat mixture evenly into the bottom of the prepared pan. Pour the peanut butter–chocolate mixture on top of the oats. Top the chocolate layer evenly with the remaining oat mixture and press lightly into the chocolate.

5. Allow the bars to cool completely before cutting into squares.

Store airtight at room temperature for up to 5 days.

Tip: These bars are equally delicious cold as they are at room temperature! If you choose to serve them cold you can store them airtight in the refrigerator for up to 1 week.

Pretzel Bark

✣ Serves 12 ✣

*P*roceed with caution. This recipe is one of those snack foods that you'll start eating and won't be able to stop until you have a stomachache, a cavity, or an empty bowl. I'm telling you, people LOVE this stuff. My oldest son says it's his favorite recipe in this book and, without sounding braggy, I know he likes everything in here! The colorful sprinkles on top are just that final touch to make this a perfect party snack!

6 cups mini pretzel twists

1 cup (2 sticks) salted butter

2 cups packed light brown sugar

4 cups white chocolate chips

½ cup rainbow sprinkles

1. Preheat the oven to 350°F. Line a 10 x 15-inch rimmed baking sheet with foil and coat lightly with cooking spray.

2. Spread the pretzels evenly onto the foil. They can overlap. Set aside.

3. In a medium saucepan, combine the butter and brown sugar and bring to a boil over medium heat. Boil for 2 minutes, stirring frequently, then pour this directly over the pretzels.

4. Bake the pretzels for 10 minutes. Set aside to cool slightly.

5. In the top of a double boiler, melt the white chocolate chips over simmering water, stirring constantly. When it's just melted, remove from the heat and carefully spread it on top of the pretzels. Sprinkle the white chocolate evenly with the rainbow sprinkles.

6. Refrigerate the pretzel bark in the pan for 15 to 20 minutes, until the chocolate is set.

7. Break or cut into pieces and serve.

Store airtight at room temperature for up to 1 week.

Tip: You can even drizzle some melted dark chocolate on top to make them extra pretty.

Cake

*It's always the answer,
no matter what the question.*

Don't we all need a little more cake in our lives? Don't get me wrong, I'm not talking about sitting and eating an entire cake every night of the week . . . I mean, unless you need to, and we have all had days like that, so no judgment here. What I mean is that cake is a dessert item normally reserved for parties or special occasions. Why does someone have to have a birthday or get married to get a dang slice of cake? The world doesn't make sense. So, I am here today to urge you to eat more cake. Celebrate a random Tuesday, folks. It's a good thing.

Confetti Cake

❖ *Serves 10* ❖

*E*veryone loves a confetti cake. My homemade version is a total fan favorite recipe on my website. The cake is a little different in that I use vegetable shortening in the batter instead of butter. The reason I do this is for the cake's texture. The shortening produces a fluffier cake with a lighter texture because it's 100 percent fat; butter is about 85 percent fat, with the other 15 percent being water, which makes your cake a bit denser. Since I was going for a supersoft cake, much like the texture of the beloved boxed confetti cake mix, I opted for shortening here. If you hate the idea of shortening in your cake, you can absolutely sub in butter in equal portions, but the texture will just be a little different.

2 cups all-purpose flour

1⅓ cups sugar

3 teaspoons baking powder

1 teaspoon kosher salt

¾ cup vegetable shortening

1¼ cups 2% or whole milk

1 tablespoon vanilla extract

3 egg whites

½ cup rainbow sprinkles

1. Preheat the oven to 350°F. Coat two 8-inch round cake pans with cooking spray. Line the bottoms with rounds of parchment paper and coat again.

2. In the bowl of a stand mixer fitted with the paddle attachment, combine the flour, sugar, baking powder, and salt. Add the shortening and mix on medium speed until the mixture is combined. Add the milk and vanilla and mix on medium speed for 2 minutes, scraping the sides of the bowl as necessary.

3. Add the egg whites and continue mixing 1 to 2 more minutes, until very smooth. Stir in the sprinkles.

4. Divide the batter evenly between the prepared pans. Bake for 20 to 25 minutes, until a toothpick inserted in the center comes out clean.

5. Allow the cakes to cool in the pans for 10 minutes, then invert them onto a wire rack to cool completely before frosting.

Store airtight at room temperature for up to 3 days.

Tips: You can also bake this in a 9 x 13-inch pan. Follow all the instructions, but bake for 30 minutes, or until the center is set and a knife inserted in the middle comes out clean.

I love to top this cake with my Perfect Buttercream (page 18), Cake Batter Frosting (page 164), or Marshmallow Buttercream (page 167)!

S'mores Cake

S'mores are the dessert of summer, no doubt. Everyone has their own idea of a perfect s'more: Burn the marshmallow or patiently wait as it turns golden brown? Serve it on a graham cracker, in the traditional way, or get creative and use chocolate chip cookies instead? Replace the milk chocolate with a peanut butter cup?! ALL good ideas. I fancy myself a bit of a s'mores expert, especially since my birthday HAPPENS to fall on National S'mores Day. Yes, it's true. I have a few fun s'mores-inspired treats in this book, but this cake is really the prize. It's a honey graham cake with toasted marshmallow buttercream frosting and milk chocolate ganache drizzled over every layer. It's a showstopper, for sure.

. . . .

CAKE:

1½ cups all-purpose flour

1 cup graham flour

1½ teaspoons baking powder

1 teaspoon baking soda

1 teaspoon kosher salt

½ cup (1 stick) salted butter, at room temperature

1 cup granulated sugar

½ cup packed dark brown sugar

¼ cup vegetable oil

2 tablespoons honey

3 large eggs

1 teaspoon vanilla extract

1 cup whole milk

(ingredient list continued on next page)

1. *For the cake:* Preheat the oven to 350°F. Coat three 8-inch round cake pans with cooking spray. Line the bottoms of the pans with rounds of parchment paper and coat with cooking spray.

2. In a large bowl, whisk together the all-purpose flour, graham flour, baking powder, baking soda, and salt. Set aside.

3. In the bowl of a stand mixer fitted with the paddle attachment, mix the butter, both sugars, the oil, and honey on medium speed for 2 minutes, scraping the sides of the bowl as necessary.

4. Add the eggs and vanilla and continue mixing for 1 more minute.

5. Reduce the speed to low and add one-third of the flour mixture, followed by half of the milk, beating after each addition. Repeat this step. End with a final addition of the flour mixture. Once all the ingredients are incorporated mix for an additional 30 seconds, until the batter is smooth.

6. Divide the batter evenly among the 3 prepared pans.

7. Bake the cakes for 20 to 25 minutes, until the center is set and a toothpick inserted in the middle comes out clean.

8. Allow the cakes to cool in the pans for 10 minutes, then invert them onto a wire rack to cool completely before frosting, peeling off the parchment paper.

(recipe continued on next page)

TOASTED MARSHMALLOW BUTTERCREAM:

1 cup (2 sticks) salted butter, at room temperature

4 cups powdered sugar

2 tablespoons whole milk

10 ounces mini marshmallows

MILK CHOCOLATE GANACHE:

2 cups chopped milk chocolate

½ cup heavy cream

Optional garnish: mini marshmallows and broken graham crackers

9. *For the toasted marshmallow buttercream:* In the bowl of a stand mixer fitted with the paddle attachment, beat the butter on medium speed for 1 minute until smooth. Turn the speed to low and slowly beat in the powdered sugar. Add the milk and continue mixing until smooth. Set aside.

10. Turn the oven to broil. Line a large baking sheet with parchment paper and spread the marshmallows out in an even layer. Place the pan under the broiler for 30 to 45 seconds, until the marshmallows are browned and puffed. Watch closely because they will burn very quickly. Immediately scrape the marshmallows into the butter mixture and beat until smooth. There will be bits of toasted marshmallows throughout the frosting; this is okay.

11. The frosting will be warm because of the broiled marshmallows, so allow it to cool completely (15 to 20 minutes) before spreading on the cake.

12. *For the milk chocolate ganache:* Place the chocolate in a heat-proof medium bowl and set aside. In a small saucepan, heat the heavy cream over medium heat until it starts to steam, stirring constantly. (Alternatively, you can heat the cream in the microwave until very hot.) Immediately pour the hot cream over the chocolate and stir until the chocolate is melted. Allow this to cool for 10 to 15 minutes, until the chocolate is thickened slightly.

13. To assemble the cake, frost the top of each cake layer with equal portions of the buttercream. Place the bottom layer onto a cake plate. Pour one-third of the ganache mixture on top of the frosting and spread it to the edge, using an offset spatula or spoon. Place the next cake layer on top of the chocolate and repeat the process. Finally, place the last cake layer on. If desired, garnish with graham cracker pieces and mini marshmallows. Drizzle the remaining ganache on top.

Store airtight until ready to serve. Keep the cake airtight at room temperature for up to 2 days.

Tip: Graham flour is a type of whole wheat flour that is used in graham crackers. I love the nutty flavor it gives to the cake, really mimicking a graham cracker. My local supermarkets carry graham flour, but if you can't seem to find it you can substitute whole wheat flour for it in this recipe.

Billionaire Cookie Dough Cake

❧ Serves 10 ❧

*I*t would be an understatement to say that this is a special-occasion cake. It is, actually, the "specialest" of special-occasion cakes. Completely over-the-top with a buttery cake base, a layer of egg-free cookie dough, homemade caramel sauce, fluffy chocolate Swiss meringue buttercream, chocolate ganache, AND buttery shortbread crumb, this one is a literal mouthful. I like to prep the ingredients for this cake the day before, because it has a few steps and prepping ahead absolutely makes this easier to put together and means you aren't stuck in the kitchen all day. The caramel, the cookie dough, and the shortbread can all be done days in advance, which is a great option! But I'll tell you, all the steps are absolutely worth it. The finished result is spectacular.

. . . .

The Essential Vanilla Cake
  (page 17)

1 cup My Favorite Caramel
  Sauce (page 159), at room
  temperature

SHORTBREAD CRUMBS:

1½ cups all-purpose flour

2 tablespoons granulated sugar

½ teaspoon kosher salt

½ cup (1 stick) salted butter,
  melted

EGG-FREE COOKIE DOUGH:

½ cup (1 stick) salted butter, at
  room temperature

¾ cup packed light brown sugar

1 teaspoon vanilla extract

1 cup all-purpose flour

2 tablespoons whole milk

¾ cup mini semisweet
  chocolate chips

(ingredient list continued on next page)

1. Bake the vanilla cake in three 8-inch cake pans as directed and allow the layers to cool completely.

2. Prepare the caramel sauce and allow it to cool as well.

3. *For the shortbread crumbs:* Preheat the oven to 350°F. Line a baking sheet with parchment paper.

4. In a medium bowl, combine the flour, granulated sugar, and salt. Stir in the melted butter until combined. Form the mixture into large crumbs and spread on the prepared baking sheet. Bake for 15 to 20 minutes, until the crumbs are golden. Allow them to cool completely on the baking sheet.

5. *For the egg-free cookie dough:* In the bowl of a stand mixer fitted with the paddle attachment, mix the butter and brown sugar on medium speed for 1 minute. Add the vanilla and mix until combined. Turn the speed to low and add the flour and milk. Mix until the dough comes together. Stir in the chocolate chips.

6. *For the chocolate Swiss meringue buttercream:* In a heatproof medium bowl, whisk together the egg whites and granulated sugar. Place the bowl over a small saucepan of one inch of simmering water (the bowl should not be touching the water). Whisk the egg whites constantly over the simmering water until the sugar has dissolved, 4 to 5 minutes.

(recipe continued on next page)

CHOCOLATE SWISS MERINGUE BUTTERCREAM:

3 large egg whites

1 cup granulated sugar

1 cup (2 sticks) salted butter, cubed, at room temperature

4 ounces semisweet chocolate chips, melted

CHOCOLATE GANACHE:

1 cup finely chopped dark chocolate

⅓ cup heavy cream

7. Immediately transfer the mixture to the bowl of a stand mixer fitted with the whisk attachment. Beat the egg whites on high speed for 10 minutes until glossy and cooled, and stiff peaks form. Add the cubed butter and continue mixing on medium speed until combined. When the butter is incorporated and the frosting is smooth, stir in the melted chocolate until incorporated.

8. To assemble the cake, dividing evenly, spread the cookie dough on the tops of 2 of the cake layers. When you're spreading the cookie dough leave the edges thicker than the center, to keep the caramel sauce from dripping down the sides of the cake.

9. Dividing evenly, spread or pour the caramel sauce on top of the cookie dough. You might need to heat up the caramel slightly so it's spreadable.

10. Refrigerate the 2 cake layers for 10 minutes to set the caramel.

11. Place one of the caramel-topped layers on a cake plate. Carefully top with the other caramel-topped layer. Top this with the remaining plain layer of cake. Using an offset spatula, cover the entire cake with the meringue buttercream.

12. *For the chocolate ganache:* Place the chocolate in a heatproof medium bowl. In a small saucepan, heat the cream over medium heat until it starts to steam, stirring constantly. (Alternatively, you can heat the cream in the microwave until very hot.) Immediately pour the hot cream on top of the chocolate and stir until the chocolate is melted. Allow this to cool for 10 to 15 minutes, until the chocolate is thickened slightly.

13. Spread the ganache on the top of the cake and allow it to drip down the sides. Top the cake with the shortbread crumbs.

Store at room temperature airtight for up to 3 days.

Egg-Free Vanilla Cupcakes

❖ *Makes 24 cupcakes* ❖

*T*his recipe for cupcakes is actually one of my favorites. The fact that they are egg-free is really a nonissue. I mean, the recipe is perfect for those with any sort of egg allergy, but honestly it's just a really great cupcake! Top these with any frosting that you like, but Creamy Chocolate Frosting (page 155) is always a good idea.

. . . .

3 cups cake flour

½ teaspoon kosher salt

2½ teaspoons baking powder

½ cup (1 stick) salted butter, at room temperature

1½ cups granulated sugar

1½ cups whole milk

2 teaspoons vanilla extract

1. Preheat the oven to 350°F. Line muffin tins with paper liners.

2. In a large bowl, whisk together the flour, salt, and baking powder. Set aside.

3. In the bowl of a stand mixer fitted with the paddle attachment, mix the butter and sugar on medium speed for 2 minutes.

4. In a separate bowl, stir the milk and vanilla together.

5. With the mixer speed on low, add one-third of the flour mixture, followed by half of the milk mixture, beating after each addition. Repeat this step. End with a final addition of the flour mixture. Beat the batter for 1 minute on medium speed, scraping the sides of the bowl as necessary.

6. Fill the muffin cups two-thirds full with batter. Bake for 20 minutes, or until the centers are set and a toothpick inserted in the middle of a cupcake comes out clean.

7. Transfer the cupcakes to a wire rack to cool completely.

Store airtight at room temperature for up to 3 days.

Hot Fudge Sundae Cake

❖ Serves 10 to 12 ❖

I, Shelly Jaronsky, have a confession to make: Of all sweets, ice cream is one of my least favorite. I know, I KNOW, but hear me out! Don't get me wrong, I really LIKE it, but if I had to rank desserts, I will always choose a cookie or a cupcake over ice cream. I'm the girl who digs through her Ben & Jerry's panning for chocolate chip cookie dough bits, eats all the goodies, and leaves a bowl of plain vanilla to die a slow, melty death. But of course I know ice cream is this whole thing that people love, so this recipe has legitimately solved my problem. Yes, there is ice cream involved, but it's on top of the fudgiest cake imaginable and topped with homemade hot fudge sauce to boot. This is the best ice cream cake I've ever had, if I do say so myself!

¾ cup all-purpose flour

1 cup granulated sugar

½ cup unsweetened cocoa powder

¾ teaspoon baking soda

½ teaspoon kosher salt

1 large egg

2 teaspoons vanilla extract

½ cup buttermilk (*DIY option page 25*)

½ cup brewed coffee, warm

4 tablespoons (½ stick) butter, melted

2 quarts vanilla ice cream

1 cup Ridiculous Hot Fudge Sauce (page 172)

15 Oreo cookies, crushed

½ cup heavy cream

2 tablespoons powdered sugar

Optional garnish: mini ice cream cones and cherries

1. Preheat the oven to 350°F. Coat a 9-inch springform pan with cooking spray.

2. In the bowl of a stand mixer fitted with the whisk attachment, mix together the flour, granulated sugar, cocoa powder, baking soda, and salt for 1 minute or until combined evenly.

3. Add the egg, vanilla, and buttermilk, mixing on medium speed until combined. Slowly add the warm coffee and melted butter, mixing until incorporated. The batter will be thin.

4. Pour the batter into the prepared pan and bake for 25 minutes, or until the center of the cake is set.

5. Allow the cake to cool completely in the pan.

6. Remove the ice cream from the freezer 15 minutes before assembling the cake.

7. With the cake still in the pan, spread ¾ cup hot fudge sauce on top of the cake. Next, sprinkle the crushed Oreo crumbs on top of the hot fudge. Spread the ice cream on top of the crushed Oreos. Drizzle the remaining ¼ cup hot fudge on top of the ice cream, cover the pan with foil, and place in the freezer for at least 3 hours or overnight.

8. When you are ready to serve the cake, in the bowl of a stand mixer fitted with the whisk attachment, whip the heavy cream and powdered sugar together until stiff peaks form.

9. Spread or pipe the whipped cream on top of the cake and garnish with mini ice cream cones and cherries, if desired.

Store airtight in the freezer for up to 1 month.

Salted Caramel Cupcakes

❧ *Makes 18 cupcakes* ❧

*T*hese salted caramel cupcakes are without a doubt my most favorite cupcake on my website. The salty/sweet/buttery combination can't be topped, and I have to say the cupcakes alone are so soft and fluffy you could enjoy them with or without all the caramel. Okay, forget I just said that . . . caramel is *always* a good idea. There are a few steps that go into making these, but the result is oh-so-perfect and definitely worth the effort.

QUICK CARAMEL SAUCE:

¾ cup (1½ sticks) salted butter

2¼ cups packed light brown sugar

¾ cup 2% or whole milk

CUPCAKES:

1¾ cups all-purpose flour

1½ teaspoons baking powder

1 teaspoon kosher salt

¾ cup (1½ sticks) salted butter, at room temperature

1½ cups granulated sugar

3 large eggs

2 teaspoons vanilla extract

¾ cup 2% or whole milk

CARAMEL BUTTERCREAM:

3 cups powdered sugar

4 tablespoons (½ stick) salted butter, at room temperature

2 tablespoons 2% or whole milk

Flaked sea salt, for garnish

1. *For the caramel sauce:* In a large saucepan, combine the butter, brown sugar, and milk and bring to a boil over medium heat, stirring frequently. Allow the mixture to boil for 3 minutes without stirring, then remove it from the heat and let it cool. The caramel will seem very thin, but it's okay. It will thicken as it cools, but you need it to be thinner than usual to soak into the cupcakes. Measure out and set aside ¾ cup caramel sauce to use in the buttercream.

2. *For the cupcakes:* Preheat the oven to 350°F. Line a muffin tin with paper liners.

3. In a large bowl, whisk together the flour, baking powder, and salt. Set aside.

4. In the bowl of a stand mixer fitted with the paddle attachment, mix the butter and granulated sugar on medium speed for 3 minutes. Add the eggs and vanilla and continue mixing until the mixture is smooth, scraping the sides of the bowl as necessary.

5. Turn the speed to low and add the flour mixture and milk at the same time, beating until the ingredients are just combined.

6. Fill each muffin cup two-thirds full with batter and bake for 20 minutes, or until a toothpick inserted in the center comes out clean. Remove the cupcakes from the pan and transfer to a wire rack to cool completely before frosting.

7. *For the caramel buttercream:* In the bowl of a stand mixer fitted with the paddle attachment, combine the reserved ¾ cup caramel sauce, the powdered sugar, butter, and milk and mix for 2 minutes until creamy, scraping the sides of the bowl as necessary.

8. To assemble the cupcakes, pierce the tops with a sharp knife or skewer 10 times. Pour 1 tablespoon of the caramel sauce on top of each cupcake, allowing it to soak into the holes.

9. Frost each cupcake with 2 to 3 tablespoons of the caramel buttercream. Drizzle the cupcakes with more caramel sauce, if desired, and lightly sprinkle the cupcakes with sea salt to garnish.

Store airtight at room temperature for up to 3 days.

Tip: You will be making 2½ cups of caramel sauce, so you can be generous on your drizzle and still have a little bit left over.

Supersoft Coconut-Lime Cake

✤ Serves 12 ✤

So yep, this is the second recipe in this book with the coconut/lime combo. Ain't no shame. I did think twice about including this recipe, because I didn't want to bore you with the same stuff, but I felt like this was just too good not to share. Popular flavor combinations make delicious recipes, and that's the whole point, isn't it?! The citrus in this cake is a standout, and in my opinion the best part. The lime pairs so well with the soft white cake and the outstanding whipped coconut buttercream. And it's limes, so like, hello mandatory daily fruit serving. It's basically like eating an apple. You're welcome.

CAKE:

2¼ cups cake flour

4 teaspoons baking powder

1 teaspoon kosher salt

1½ cups granulated sugar

6 large egg whites

½ cup coconut milk

½ cup whole milk

1 teaspoon vanilla extract

2 teaspoons grated lime zest

¼ cup lime juice

¾ cup (1½ sticks) salted butter, melted and cooled slightly

LIME SYRUP:

1 cup granulated sugar

¼ cup lime juice

¼ cup water

WHIPPED COCONUT BUTTERCREAM FROSTING:

1 cup (2 sticks) salted butter, at room temperature

3 cups powdered sugar

¼ cup coconut milk

2 cups shredded sweetened coconut

1. *For the cake:* Preheat the oven to 350°F. Coat a 9 x 13-inch baking dish with cooking spray.

2. In the bowl of a stand mixer fitted with the paddle attachment, stir together the flour, baking powder, salt, and granulated sugar.

3. In a separate medium bowl, whisk together the egg whites, coconut milk, dairy milk, vanilla, lime zest, and lime juice until combined and smooth.

4. With the mixer on low speed, slowly add the melted butter to the flour mixture until combined. Still on low speed, slowly add the egg/milk mixture until combined. Turn the mixer up slowly to medium and mix the batter for 2 minutes. If a few lumps remain, this is fine.

5. Pour the batter into the prepared pan and bake for 35 to 40 minutes until a toothpick inserted in the center comes out clean.

6. *Meanwhile, for the lime syrup:* In a small saucepan, combine the granulated sugar, lime juice, and water and bring to a boil over medium heat. Boil the syrup for 5 minutes. Remove from the heat and allow to cool slightly.

7. When the cake is done, remove it from the oven and, using a knife, poke holes all over the top of the cake. Pour the syrup onto the cake and allow the cake to cool completely in the pan.

8. *Meanwhile, for the whipped coconut buttercream frosting:* In the bowl of a stand mixer fitted with the paddle attachment, mix the butter on medium speed for 1 minute or until smooth. Turn the speed to low and slowly add the powdered sugar until combined. Slowly pour in the coconut milk, turn the speed up to medium, and mix for 1 minute.

9. When the cake is cooled, frost the top of the cake in the pan. Sprinkle evenly with shredded coconut.

Store airtight at room temperature for up to 3 days.

Tip: If you don't love lime, you can easily sub in any other citrus fruit like lemon or even orange, which would complement the coconut perfectly!

Banana Cupcakes

✣ Makes 20 cupcakes ✣

*T*hese are the softest cupcakes you'll ever eat. They're loaded with banana flavor and they bake up like a dream! I love serving these with Cream Cheese Frosting (page 160), as shown here, but topping them with Browned Butter Frosting (page 175) or Marshmallow Buttercream (page 167) would be unexpected and delicious! I haven't met a single person who doesn't love these cupcakes.

½ cup (1 stick) salted butter, at room temperature

1 cup packed light brown sugar

¼ cup granulated sugar

2 large eggs

1 teaspoon vanilla extract

1 heaping cup mashed banana (about 3 very ripe medium bananas)

¼ cup buttermilk (*DIY option page 25*)

1 teaspoon baking powder

½ teaspoon baking soda

½ teaspoon salt

2 cups all-purpose flour

1. Preheat the oven to 350°F. Line a muffin tin with paper liners.

2. In the bowl of a stand mixer fitted with the paddle attachment, mix the butter and both sugars on medium speed for 2 minutes. Add the eggs, vanilla, mashed banana, and buttermilk, continuing to mix until evenly incorporated and smooth, scraping the sides of the bowl as necessary. With the mixer still running, add the baking powder, baking soda, and salt and mix until combined.

3. Turn the speed to low and add the flour, mixing until just incorporated.

4. Fill the muffin cups two-thirds full with batter. Bake for 20 minutes, or until a toothpick inserted into the center comes out clean. Allow the cupcakes to cool for 5 minutes in the muffin tin, then transfer to a wire rack to cool completely before frosting.

Store airtight at room temperature for up to 2 days.

Brown Sugar Cupcakes

❧ *Makes 12 cupcakes* ❧

*I*f you haven't noticed already, I am a bit of a brown sugar fanatic. The rich flavor and the softness that the added touch of molasses in the sugar gives to baked goods . . . ahh, there are just no words. Adding brown sugar to cake batter seems like the obvious choice to my little brain. The outcome is an ultrasoft, flavor-packed cupcake that will leave you questioning granulated sugar's very existence.

1⅓ cups all-purpose flour

½ teaspoon baking powder

½ teaspoon baking soda

½ teaspoon kosher salt

¾ cup (1½ sticks) salted butter, at room temperature

¾ cup packed light brown sugar

2 large eggs

½ cup whole milk

1 teaspoon vanilla extract

1. Preheat the oven to 350°F. Line 12 cups of a muffin tin with paper liners.

2. In a large bowl, whisk together the flour, baking powder, baking soda, and salt. Set aside.

3. In the bowl of a stand mixer fitted with the paddle attachment, mix the butter and brown sugar on medium speed for 2 minutes until light and fluffy.

4. With the mixer still on medium, add the eggs and mix for 1 minute until combined and smooth, scraping the sides of the bowl as necessary.

5. In a measuring cup, mix together the milk and the vanilla.

6. Turn the mixer speed to low and add one-third of the flour mixture, followed by half of the milk, beating after each addition. Repeat this step. End with a final addition of the flour mixture. Mix until the batter is smooth.

7. Fill the muffin cups two-thirds full with batter. Bake for 15 to 20 minutes or until a toothpick inserted in the center comes out clean.

8. Remove the cupcakes from the pan and transfer to a wire rack to cool completely before frosting.

Store airtight at room temperature for up to 3 days.

Tip: I love this cupcake topped with Browned Butter Frosting (page 175).

Banana Blondie–Bottomed Cheesecake

❧ *Serves 12* ❧

*J*f I had to choose a single dessert as my favorite, it would be cheesecake. Of course my most favorite is a cheesecake that sits on top of a thick, buttery, graham cracker crust, but I'm always looking to up my cheesecake game . . . and if that means making a soft, brown sugar, banana blondie and placing a thick layer of cheesecake on top of that, with a healthy dose of salted caramel in between . . . well, I'm willing to step up. Because I love you guys. And someone's got to.

CHEESECAKE:

3 (8-ounce) packages cream cheese, at room temperature

1 cup granulated sugar

3 large eggs

2 teaspoons vanilla extract

¾ cup sour cream

½ cup whole milk

3 tablespoons all-purpose flour

BLONDIE:

½ cup (1 stick) salted butter, melted

1 cup packed light brown sugar

1 large egg

1½ teaspoons vanilla extract

¼ teaspoon kosher salt

1 cup all-purpose flour

½ cup mashed banana, about 2 small bananas

ASSEMBLY:

1¼ cups caramel sauce, store-bought or My Favorite Caramel Sauce (page 159)

3 teaspoons flaked sea salt

1. *For the cheesecake:* Preheat the oven to 350°F. Coat a 9-inch springform pan with cooking spray.

2. In the bowl of a stand mixer fitted with the paddle attachment, mix the cream cheese and granulated sugar on medium-low speed for 1 to 2 minutes until smooth. With the mixer still on medium-low speed, add the eggs and vanilla, mixing until smooth, scraping the sides and the bottom of the bowl as necessary.

3. Turn the speed to low and slowly mix in the sour cream and milk until incorporated. Add the flour and mix to combine.

4. Pour the cheesecake mixture into the prepared pan. Bake for 1 hour, or until the cheesecake is almost set. The center will still be slightly loose. Turn the oven off and allow the cheesecake to remain in the oven for 2 more hours without opening the door.

5. Remove the cheesecake from the oven, cover, and refrigerate for 4 hours or overnight.

6. *For the blondie:* Preheat the oven to 350°F. Coat a 9-inch round cake pan with cooking spray. Line the bottom of the pan with a round of parchment paper and coat the parchment with cooking spray.

7. In the bowl of a stand mixer fitted with the paddle attachment, mix the melted butter and brown sugar on medium speed until combined. Add the egg and vanilla and mix on medium speed until smooth. Turn the mixer speed to low and add in the salt and flour until just combined. Mix in the banana until incorporated.

8. Spread the batter in the prepared pan. Bake for 25 minutes, or until a toothpick inserted 3 inches from the edge comes out clean.

9. Allow the blondie to cool in the pan.

10. *To assemble the cheesecake:* Remove the blondie from the pan and transfer it to a cake plate. Spread ¾ cup of the caramel sauce over the blondie. Sprinkle the caramel with 1 teaspoon of the flaked sea salt.

11. Carefully remove the cheesecake from the pan by sliding a large spatula under the cheesecake and placing it onto the caramel-coated blondie. Spread the remaining ¾ cup caramel sauce over the cheesecake and sprinkle with the remaining 2 teaspoons sea salt.

12. Serve immediately or cover and refrigerate until you're ready to serve.

Store airtight in the refrigerator for up to 3 days.

Adaptable Dump Cake

❧ Serves 10 ❧

*D*ump cakes are one of those retro desserts that a lot of us grew up eating. Recently they have regained a bit of popularity, which I have to say thrills me. The wonderful thing about this unfortunately named dessert is that it's basically impossible to mess up. Not only that, but you can really get creative with your favorite fruit filling combinations! So don't be afraid to be bold when you're making this rich, buttery cobbler. And of course, for the love of all that is good and fair in this world, serve it with ice cream!

. . . .

1 (21-ounce) can fruit pie filling

2 cups fresh or thawed frozen fruit (chopped into bite-size pieces if you use a large fruit)

1 (15.25-ounce) box yellow cake mix

½ cup coarse graham cracker crumbs or chopped nuts

½ cup (1 stick) salted butter, cubed

1. Preheat the oven to 350°F. Coat a 9 x 13-inch baking dish with cooking spray.

2. Pour the pie filling into the baking dish and sprinkle the chopped fruit evenly on top of the pie filling. Sprinkle the fruit with the dry cake mix and then the graham cracker crumbs. Top the cake mix evenly with cubed butter.

3. Bake for 45 minutes until the top is golden and the fruit is bubbly.

4. Serve warm or at room temperature.

Store airtight at room temperature for up to 2 days.

Tip: I like the combination of mixed berry pie filling and fresh strawberries or blueberries! You can also get creative and use an apple pie filling with chunks of fresh Granny Smith apples and a handful of raisins thrown in for a supremely fall version of this dump cake.

Caramel Apple Upside Down Cake

❧ Serves 10 ❧

*M*y cast-iron skillet makes as much dessert as it does dinner; it's such a versatile and useful kitchen tool. One of my favorite things to make in the skillet is cake! I LOVE caramel apple anything, and when you bake the cake upside down in the skillet, you'll get chewy caramel edges and soft cake. Need I say more?

CARAMEL APPLE TOPPING:

¾ cup (1½ sticks) salted butter

¾ cup packed light brown sugar

2 small Granny Smith apples, peeled and cut into ½-inch-thick slices

CAKE:

1½ cups all-purpose flour

½ teaspoon ground cinnamon

2 teaspoons baking powder

½ teaspoon kosher salt

¾ cup (1½ sticks) salted butter, at room temperature

1 cup granulated sugar

2 large eggs

2 teaspoons vanilla extract

½ cup sweetened or unsweetened applesauce

1. Preheat the oven to 350°F.

2. *For the caramel apple topping:* In a 10-inch cast-iron skillet, melt the butter over medium heat. Add the brown sugar and bring the mixture to a boil. Boil for 3 minutes, stirring constantly. Remove the skillet from the heat and arrange the apple slices evenly in a circular pattern until the bottom of the pan is covered with apples. Set aside.

3. *For the cake:* In a bowl, whisk together the flour, cinnamon, baking powder, and salt. Set aside.

4. In the bowl of a stand mixer fitted with the paddle attachment, beat the butter and granulated sugar on medium speed for 2 minutes until light and fluffy, scraping the sides of the bowl as necessary.

5. Add the eggs and vanilla and continue mixing at medium speed, until smooth.

6. Turn the speed to low and add half of the flour mixture, mixing until incorporated. Next add the applesauce and mix until combined. Add the remaining flour mixture and mix until just incorporated. Do not overmix the batter.

7. Spoon the batter on top of the apple layer and place the skillet in the oven. Bake for 35 to 40 minutes, until a toothpick inserted in the center comes out clean.

8. Remove the skillet from the oven and allow to cool for 5 minutes. Invert the skillet onto a serving dish.

9. Serve warm.

Tip: Top with ice cream, whipped cream, or extra caramel sauce, either store-bought or homemade (see My Favorite Caramel Sauce, page 159).

Peppermint Pattie Cake

❧ Serves 12 ❧

*T*his cake is a showstopper, no question. The dark devil's food cake layers juxtaposed with the cool, bright-white minty frosting is simply stunning, not to mention majorly tasty. Topping all of that with a delicious and dramatic dark chocolate ganache and a mound of Peppermint Pattie candies is enough to make my heart swoon. I have to say it's almost too pretty to eat, but that would be ridiculous—this cake is way too rich and soft to go untouched! The frosting is subtly minty, just enough to offset the decadence of the chocolate. It's a match made in heaven!

CAKE:

2 cups cake flour

2 cups granulated sugar

1 cup unsweetened cocoa powder

2 teaspoons baking powder

1 teaspoon baking soda

1 teaspoon kosher salt

1 cup vegetable oil

1 cup brewed coffee, cooled

1 cup buttermilk (*DIY option page 25*)

2 large eggs

2 teaspoons vanilla extract

PEPPERMINT CREAM CHEESE FROSTING:

1 cup (2 sticks) salted butter, at
   room temperature

4 ounces cream cheese, at room
   temperature

8 cups powdered sugar

2 teaspoons peppermint extract

DARK CHOCOLATE GANACHE:

1 cup finely chopped dark chocolate

⅓ cup heavy cream

Peppermint Patties, for garnish

1. *For the cake:* Preheat the oven to 325°F. Coat three 9-inch round cake pans with cooking spray. Line the bottoms with rounds of parchment paper and coat the pans again with cooking spray.

2. In the bowl of a stand mixer fitted with the paddle attachment, combine the cake flour, granulated sugar, cocoa powder, baking powder, baking soda, salt, oil, coffee, buttermilk, eggs, and vanilla. With the mixer on low speed, slowly combine the ingredients. Turn the mixer up to medium and beat the batter for 3 minutes. The batter will be thin.

3. Divide the batter evenly among the 3 prepared pans. Bake for 35 minutes, or until a toothpick inserted in the center comes out clean.

4. Allow the cakes to cool in the pans for 5 minutes, then invert them onto a wire rack to cool completely before frosting.

5. *For the peppermint cream cheese frosting:* In the bowl of a stand mixer fitted with the paddle attachment, mix the butter and cream cheese on medium speed for 2 minutes or until smooth.

6. Turn the speed to low and slowly add the powdered sugar until incorporated, then turn the speed up to medium and beat the frosting for 2 minutes. Add the peppermint extract and beat for an additional 30 seconds.

7. *For the dark chocolate ganache:* Place the chocolate in a heatproof medium bowl. In a small saucepan, heat the cream over medium heat until it starts to steam, stirring constantly. (Alternatively you can heat the cream in the microwave until very hot.) Immediately pour the hot cream over the chocolate and stir until the chocolate is melted. Allow this to cool for 10 to 15 minutes, until the chocolate is thickened slightly.

8. To assemble the cake, place a cake layer on a cake plate and top with one-third of the frosting. Top this with a second cake layer and frost that with another third of the frosting. Repeat for the top layer.

9. When the ganache is fully cooled, carefully spoon the ganache on top of the cake. Use an offset spatula or spoon to push the ganache to the edge of the cake so it will drip down the sides. Let the ganache set for 25 to 30 minutes and then top with as many Peppermint Patties as you like.

Store airtight at room temperature for up to 3 days.

Fruity Pebbles Cake

❖ Serves 12 ❖

*F*ruity Pebbles are my favorite cereal. Like ever. I know there isn't much nutritional value to them and they're basically dessert (which I am sure is why I love them), but I find them totally irresistible. Whether in a bowl with milk, sprinkled on top of ice cream, or (as I have done with this cake) mixed into frosting, the sweet, fruity flavor is nostalgic and comforting for me. My kids have also inherited the Fruity Pebbles gene, so a box doesn't last more than a day or two in my house. This cake is a fresh strawberry cake topped with frosting that's sweetened and colored using the happy cereal. We love it!

CAKE:

2¾ cups all-purpose flour

2½ teaspoons baking powder

½ teaspoon salt

¾ cup pureed strawberries (about 2 cups whole strawberries, fresh or thawed frozen)

1 teaspoon vanilla extract

1 cup whole milk

1 cup (2 sticks) salted butter, at room temperature

2 cups granulated sugar

4 large eggs

FROSTING:

1½ cups (3 sticks) salted butter, at room temperature

3 cups powdered sugar

3 tablespoons heavy cream

1¼ cups crushed Fruity Pebbles cereal (about 4 cups uncrushed)

Fruity Pebbles, for garnish (optional)

1. *For the cake:* Preheat the oven to 350°F. Coat a 9 x 13-inch baking dish with cooking spray.

2. In a medium bowl, whisk together the flour, baking powder, and salt. Set aside.

3. In a separate medium bowl, whisk together the strawberry puree, vanilla, and milk. Set aside.

4. In the bowl of a stand mixer fitted with the paddle attachment, mix the butter and granulated sugar on medium speed for 2 minutes. Add the eggs and continue mixing until smooth, scraping the sides of the bowl as necessary.

5. Turn the speed to low and add one-third of the flour mixture, followed by half of the strawberry mixture, beating after each addition. Repeat this step. End with a final addition of the flour mixture, mixing until smooth and scraping the sides of the bowl as necessary.

6. Pour the batter into the prepared pan. Bake for 25 to 30 minutes, until the cake is set and a toothpick inserted into the center comes out clean.

7. Allow the cake to cool completely in the pan before frosting.

8. *For the frosting:* In the bowl of a stand mixer fitted with the paddle attachment, mix the butter on medium speed until smooth. Turn the speed to low and slowly add the powdered sugar and cream, beating until smooth. Add the crushed cereal and beat about 1 minute, until smooth.

9. Spread the frosting on top of the cooled cake. If desired, garnish with a sprinkling of Fruity Pebbles.

Store airtight at room temperature for up to 2 days.

Icy Lemon Cake

❖ Serves 10 ❖

*T*his cake has a secret ingredient. Okay, it's not really secret at all. It's cake mix. Yep. Now, I know there are folks out there who stand up on the rooftops and holler their opposition to cake mixes . . . but y'all . . . we need to just leave our judgment at the dang door and understand that there's a time and place for everything. I really love cakes made from scratch, but friends, this cake wouldn't be what it is without the extra fairy dust that goes into a boxed mix. I did doctor it up with some extras, and what we are left with is a delicious, fluffy, soft, lemon cake with icy lemon frosting. It's pretty amazing.

CAKE:

1 (18.25-ounce) box white cake mix

1 cup all-purpose flour

1 cup granulated sugar

1 tablespoon grated lemon zest

1 cup water

⅓ cup lemon juice

1 cup sour cream

2 tablespoons vegetable oil

2 teaspoons vanilla extract

4 large egg whites

FROSTING:

1 cup (2 sticks) salted butter, at room temperature

6 cups powdered sugar

¼ cup lemon juice

1 teaspoon vanilla extract

Lemon slices, for garnish (optional)

1. *For the cake:* Preheat the oven to 350°F. Coat two 8-inch round cake pans with cooking spray. Line the bottoms with rounds of parchment paper and coat the paper with cooking spray.

2. In the bowl of a stand mixer fitted with the paddle attachment, mix the cake mix, flour, granulated sugar, and lemon zest on low speed for 2 minutes, until combined.

3. With the mixer still on low, add the water, lemon juice, sour cream, oil, vanilla, and egg whites and mix until combined. Turn the speed up to medium and mix for 2 minutes, scraping the sides of the bowl as necessary.

4. Divide the batter evenly between the 2 pans. Bake for 20 to 25 minutes, until a toothpick inserted in the center comes out clean.

5. Allow the cakes to cool in the pans for 10 minutes, then invert them onto a wire rack to cool completely before frosting.

6. *For the frosting:* In the bowl of a stand mixer fitted with the whisk attachment, mix the butter on medium speed for 1 minute until smooth.

7. Turn the speed down to low and mix in the powdered sugar until combined. Add the lemon juice and vanilla, turn the speed up to medium, and beat the frosting for 2 minutes until creamy.

8. Fill and cover the top and sides of the cake with the frosting. If desired, garnish with fresh lemon slices.

Store airtight at room temperature for up to 3 days.

Oatmeal Cream Pie Cookie Cake

❧ Serves 12 ❧

J would be remiss if I didn't admit to y'all that this is one crazy cake. It is, of course, based on the popular, cellophane-wrapped lunchtime snack of my childhood. But instead of just making a copycat version of the cookie sandwich, I decided to kick it up about 14 notches and make one ridiculously epic cake. The oatmeal cookies are supersoft, and the sweet marshmallow buttercream holds it all together. You can slice and serve it just like a regular cake. I'm telling you now, this might be my favorite dessert in the entire book . . . it's outrageously good!

. . . .

1 cup (2 sticks) salted butter, at room temperature

1¾ cups packed dark brown sugar

4 large eggs

2 teaspoons vanilla extract

1 teaspoon ground cinnamon

1½ teaspoons baking soda

½ teaspoon kosher salt

2 cups quick-cooking oats

2¼ cups all-purpose flour

Marshmallow Buttercream (page 167)

1. Preheat the oven to 350°F. Line a baking sheet with parchment paper.

2. In the bowl of a stand mixer fitted with the paddle attachment, mix the butter and brown sugar on medium speed for 2 minutes.

3. Add the eggs, vanilla, cinnamon, baking soda, and salt and mix on medium speed until smooth, scraping the sides of the bowl as necessary.

4. Turn the speed to low. Add the oats and the flour and mix until just combined.

5. Using a medium (2-tablespoon) cookie scoop, drop the dough 2 inches apart on the baking sheet. You should have 35 cookies.

6. Bake the cookies for 8 to 9 minutes, until lightly golden around the edges. Don't overbake them, as you need them to be soft.

7. Transfer the cookies to a wire rack to cool completely before assembling the cake.

8. To assemble the cake, divide the cookies into 5 equal portions and divide the buttercream into 5 equal portions.

9. Arrange one portion of the cookies on a cake stand or plate in a round. If they overlap, it's fine. Top them with one portion of the buttercream. Repeat this, building layers using all the cookies, ending with the buttercream.

Store airtight at room temperature for up to 3 days.

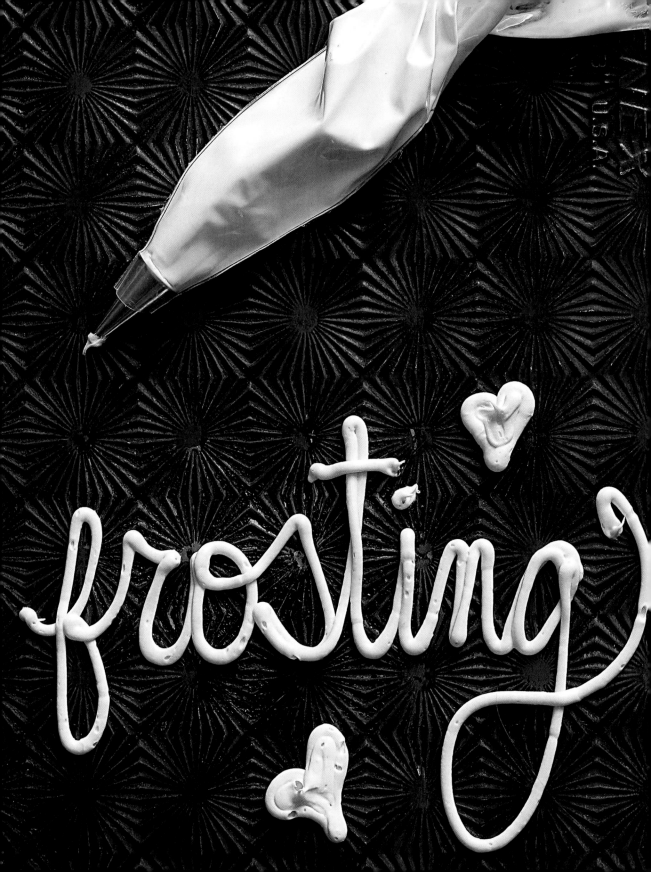

Frosting

I'll take a corner piece, please.

Let's have a heart-to-heart for a quick minute. I feel like the world is divided into two camps: those who love their frosting and those who don't. And when I say "frosting" I mean the real deal: butter, powdered sugar, and all the calories. I decidedly do NOT mean the "lighter whipped topping" that people fool themselves into thinking is better for them. I really feel that if you're going to have dessert—cake, for example—you need to HAVE cake. And eat it, too. With all the trimmings. Like really do it. Enjoy that slice, ask for a corner piece, or the largest frosting rose . . . because we all know a cake is only as good as its frosting.

Creamy Chocolate Frosting

❖ Makes 3½ cups ❖

*E*veryone needs a good chocolate frosting recipe. For years I used to crack open a tin of frosting and call it a day. Like I have said before, I'm not a judger of premade ingredients. I'm all about making your life easier, trust me. But oh, friends, please, please make your own frosting. It's incredibly easy and infinitely better than the packaged varieties. Plus, I am assuming if you're reading this book, you're all about frosting. And I love you for it.

. . . .

1 cup (2 sticks) salted butter, at room temperature

1 cup unsweetened cocoa powder

8 cups powdered sugar

1 teaspoon vanilla extract

⅔ cup very hot water

1. In the bowl of a stand mixer fitted with the paddle attachment, combine the butter, cocoa powder, powdered sugar, vanilla, and hot water and mix on low speed, until the mixture just comes together.

2. Slowly increase the speed to medium and beat the frosting for 2 minutes, scraping the sides of the bowl as necessary.

3. Let the frosting cool for 15 minutes before spreading on your cake or cupcakes.

Store airtight at room temperature for up to 3 days, refrigerated for up to 1 week, or in the freezer for up to 1 month. If refrigerated or frozen, allow the frosting to return to room temperature before using.

Tip: Use regular unsweetened cocoa powder for a lighter chocolate frosting, or use a dark cocoa powder for a deeper, fudgier frosting.

Candy Frosting

*T*his frosting recipe is one of my favorites. It's basically a blank canvas that you can change up with whatever candy suits your fancy. My boys came up with this idea and we have made so many versions of this frosting with great success! Peanut butter cups work perfectly, so do M&M's and Nestlé Crunch Bars. A gooey candy might not work as well when you try to pulverize it, so stick with firmer candy that can easily be crushed. Butterfingers are a family favorite and they happen to work perfectly. You could even mix up candies for a very customized frosting. Get creative!

. . . .

1 cup (2 sticks) salted butter, at room temperature

3 cups powdered sugar

¾ cup finely crushed candy (or candies) of your choosing

1. In the bowl of a stand mixer fitted with the paddle attachment, mix the butter on medium speed until smooth. Turn the speed to low and add the powdered sugar. Turn the mixer back up to medium and beat the frosting for 1 to 2 minutes until creamy.

2. Add the crushed candy and mix until evenly incorporated.

Store airtight at room temperature for up to 3 days, refrigerated for up to 5 days, or in the freezer for up to 1 month. If refrigerated or frozen, allow the frosting to return to room temperature before using.

Tip: I like to use my blender or food processor to pulverize the candy into a fine dust before incorporating it into the frosting.

My Favorite Caramel Sauce

❧ Makes 1½ cups ❧

*H*omemade caramel sauce is a weakness of mine. I only really got the hang of making it a few years ago, but ever since then I haven't looked back. I totally get how skimming a recipe and seeing the dreaded words "candy thermometer" sends a lot of you running for the hills. I was once you. But fear not, friends, the candy thermometer isn't that scary after all. I mean, none of us fear the meat thermometer, right? I've never once read a recipe for chicken, seen the temperature "170°F" and thought, "Nope. Not making that." Anyhow, my point is, it's not that big of a deal. If I can do it, you surely can as well.

1¼ cups granulated sugar

2 tablespoons water

7 tablespoons butter, cubed

½ cup plus 2 tablespoons heavy cream

1. In a medium saucepan, combine the sugar and water and bring to a boil over medium heat, stirring.

2. Continuing to stir frequently to ensure all the sugar dissolves, boil until the mixture reaches 350°F on a candy thermometer. As soon as it reaches 350°F, add the butter and stir until melted, then slowly add the cream, stirring until combined. The mixture will splatter and seize up slightly while adding the cream; this is okay, just keep stirring until combined. Allow the mixture to boil for 2 more minutes, watching closely and stirring often because it will bubble, and then remove from the heat immediately.

3. Allow the mixture to cool before using.

Store airtight in the refrigerator for up to 2 weeks. Reheat in the microwave or on the stovetop before using.

Tip: To make this into Salted Caramel Sauce, just add 2 teaspoons of kosher salt or flaked sea salt right when you remove the mixture from the heat. Stir it in well so it dissolves. You can adjust the amount of salt to your taste.

Cream Cheese Frosting

❖ *Makes 3 cups* ❖

*C*ream cheese frosting is a standard. A classic. It goes perfectly on just about anything, from cupcakes to pancakes to cinnamon rolls to a spoon. This recipe makes perfectly creamy frosting with the just-right amount of sweetness. It whips up quickly and makes everything it's on more delicious!

. . . .

8 ounces cream cheese, at room temperature

½ cup (1 stick) salted butter, at room temperature

4 cups powdered sugar

1 to 2 tablespoons whole milk or heavy cream

1. In the bowl of a stand mixer fitted with the paddle attachment, mix the butter and cream cheese on medium speed 1 to 2 minutes until smooth and creamy.

2. Turn the speed to low and slowly add the powdered sugar. Once incorporated, turn the speed back up to medium and continue mixing until smooth. Add 1 tablespoon of the milk or cream and continue mixing. If necessary, add an additional tablespoon of milk until the desired consistency is reached.

Store airtight in the refrigerator for up to 5 days, or in the freezer for up to 1 month. If refrigerated or frozen, allow the frosting to return to room temperature before using.

Fluffy Meringue Frosting

Makes 4 cups

*T*his frosting is the fluffiest, creamiest mother-lovin' confection ever to exist. It's super spreadable so you can use it to top cupcakes or cover cakes. It's like a fluffy marshmallow meets a cloud and, *boom!* they have a frosting baby. Too far? Sorry.

There is no fat added to this so it's actually quite light in texture, but it's sweet enough to be considered frosting. It toasts beautifully so you can get that gorgeous amber color when you take a kitchen torch to the tips. It's glossy and creamy and lovely. If you can't tell, I'm a big fan of this one.

6 large egg whites

1½ cups granulated sugar

⅛ teaspoon kosher salt

1 teaspoon vanilla extract

1. In the top of a double boiler, whisk together the egg whites, sugar, salt, and vanilla. Heat the egg white mixture over the simmering water, stirring constantly, until the mixture reaches 140°F on a candy thermometer.

2. Immediately pour the mixture into the bowl of a stand mixer fitted with the whisk attachment. Beat on high speed for 8 to 10 minutes, until stiff, glossy peaks form.

This frosting is best if used immediately.

Cake Batter Frosting

❖ *Makes 1½ cups* ❖

*S*prinkles make people happy. I am fairly sure that is a scientifically proven fact. Adding not only sprinkles but dry cake mix as well into a creamy buttery frosting takes happy and multiplies it by 1,000. This frosting is perfect on any flavor of cake, on top of brownies, or even sandwiched between two graham crackers. I dare you to find someone who doesn't love this.

1 cup (2 sticks) salted butter, at room temperature

½ cup dry vanilla cake mix

3 cups powdered sugar

1 tablespoon heavy cream

¼ cup rainbow sprinkles

1. In the bowl of a stand mixer fitted with the paddle attachment, mix the butter on medium speed until smooth. Turn the speed to low and add the cake mix, powdered sugar, and heavy cream, mixing until just combined. Turn the speed back up to medium and beat for an additional minute, until the frosting is smooth and creamy.

2. Add the sprinkles and mix on low speed until incorporated.

Store airtight at room temperature for up to 2 days, refrigerated for up to 5 days, or in the freezer for up to 1 month. If refrigerated or frozen, allow the frosting to return to room temperature before using.

Marshmallow Buttercream

*T*his fun spin on traditional buttercream is so creamy and sweet. Combining the Marshmallow Fluff with the butter creates a different texture that I just adore. Substitute this frosting out wherever you would normally use plain vanilla frosting—people will love the little switch even if they can't place what you've done. It's like sneaking spinach into brownies when trying to trick your kids into eating their veggies. Except the complete opposite.

1 cup (2 sticks) salted butter, at room temperature

14 ounces Marshmallow Fluff

2 cups powdered sugar

In the bowl of a stand mixer fitted with the paddle attachment, mix the butter on medium speed until smooth. Add the marshmallow crème and mix on medium speed until smooth. Turn the speed to low and slowly add the powdered sugar until combined. Turn the speed back up to medium and beat until smooth.

Store airtight at room temperature for up to 2 days, in the refrigerator for up to 5 days, or in the freezer for up to 1 month. If refrigerated or frozen, allow the frosting to return to room temperature before using.

Brownie Batter Frosting

❧ Makes 3 cups ❧

This frosting recipe is SUPER over-the-top. It's basically one giant hyperbole. BEST. AMAZING. FAVORITE. Is this a necessary frosting recipe in your life? Depends on your definition of "necessary." But once you make this creamy, rich, and decadent frosting you will want to spread it all over your Monday morning.

. . . .

1 cup (2 sticks) salted butter, at room temperature

1 cup dry brownie mix

1 cup powdered sugar

¼ cup heavy cream

1. In the bowl of a stand mixer fitted with the paddle attachment, mix the butter and brownie mix on medium-high speed until creamy and smooth. Turn the speed to low and add the powdered sugar, mixing until incorporated. The mixture will be dry.

2. With the mixer still on low, slowly stream in the cream and mix until combined. Turn the speed back up to medium-high and beat for 1 to 2 minutes until the frosting is creamy and smooth, scraping the sides of the bowl as necessary.

Store airtight at room temperature for up to 2 days, or refrigerated for up to 5 days, or in the freezer for up to 1 month. If refrigerated or frozen, allow the frosting to return to room temperature before using.

Glaze Icing

*F*rom my early baking days spent making and decorating sugar cookies, I learned that decorating cookies requires a good amount of time and patience. And unfortunately (okay, fortunately), I was always more interested in EATING the cookies than I was in making them look pretty. So while my decorating days are over, my eating days are still in full swing. And I learned that making a pourable glaze icing to coat cookies and cakes is not only delicious, but can also be really beautiful. The great thing about this glaze icing is that it's creamy and sweet, but you can easily make it thicker and use it to pipe beautiful borders, or thin it out so you can flood the cookie for a smooth and glossy finish. You can color it with any food coloring or gel, and you can whip it up in a pinch to pour over a Bundt cake. So many possibilities!

- -

2 cups powdered sugar

½ cup heavy cream

3 tablespoons 2% or whole milk

1 teaspoon vanilla extract

In a medium bowl, combine the powdered sugar, cream, milk, and vanilla and whisk until the icing is smooth. You can add more milk if you would like a thinner icing, or less for a thicker icing.

Store airtight in the refrigerator for up to 3 days.

Ridiculous Hot Fudge Sauce

❖ *Makes 4 cups* ❖

*H*ot fudge sauce is truly nostalgic for me. It brings back lots of childhood memories of ice cream sundae desserts made with my parents and grandparents. We even had a dog named Fudge, appropriately named for our favorite ice cream topping. I'm serious. Usually we just grabbed a jar of ready-made fudge topping from the refrigerator and heated it up in the microwave to top our vanilla sundaes, but every once in a while my grandma would make a special homemade hot fudge that could NOT be beat. This is one of the recipes that I got from her recipe box. It's rich, chocolaty, and simple, and you're going to love it!

· ·

13 tablespoons salted
  butter, cut into cubes

⅓ cup unsweetened cocoa
  powder

4 ounces bittersweet
  chocolate, chopped

1 cup granulated sugar

1 cup packed light brown
  sugar

1 (12-ounce) can
  evaporated milk

2 teaspoons vanilla extract

¼ teaspoon salt

1. In a medium saucepan, combine the butter, cocoa powder, chocolate, both sugars, and evaporated milk. Stirring, bring to a boil over medium heat. Allow to boil for 5 minutes, stirring frequently.

2. Remove from the heat and stir in the vanilla and salt. Transfer the sauce to a blender and blend for 3 minutes.

3. Serve warm.

Store airtight in the refrigerator for up to 1 week. Reheat in the microwave or on the stovetop.

Browned Butter Frosting

*T*his frosting is terrifically life changing. The simple extra step takes a regular butter frosting to new heights. It's richer and deeper in flavor and infinitely more interesting than its standard counterpart. I am fairly certain you will want to brown butter in every recipe you have from here on out. Like I said, life changing.

. . . .

1 cup (2 sticks) salted butter

4 cups powdered sugar

1 teaspoon vanilla extract

¼ to ⅓ cup whole milk

1. In a medium saucepan, bring the butter to a boil over medium heat. Once it starts boiling, swirl the pan constantly until the butter passes the foamy phase and becomes a deep amber color. Remove the pot from the heat and refrigerate the butter for at least 1 hour, until it becomes solid again. (You can do this in the same pan or transfer it into a smaller container.)

2. Once the butter is solid, transfer it to the bowl of a stand mixer fitted with the paddle attachment. Allow it to come back to room temperature.

3. With the mixer on low speed, add the powdered sugar, vanilla, and ¼ cup of milk until combined. Turn the speed up to medium and beat for 1 to 2 minutes. You can add more powdered sugar or more milk to achieve the consistency you desire.

Store airtight at room temperature for up to 2 days, in the refrigerator for up to 5 days, or in the freezer for up to 1 month. If refrigerated or frozen, allow the frosting to return to room temperature before using.

Marshmallow Fondant

Makes enough to cover a 9-inch layer cake, with extra for decorations

*W*ait! Before you skip over this deceptively easy recipe because you "don't like fondant," just give me one minute of your time. Look, I get it: Fondant isn't buttercream, and when a cake isn't frosted in buttercream, I, too, turn and walk the other way in a disgusted huff. We've all been to that wedding or birthday party where they roll out the most beautiful cake covered in fondant. We all ooh and ahh over its gorgeousness . . . and then we all take a bite and push it to the side because gross. Most fondant kind of sucks, I get it. But not on my watch, friends. This fondant is ridiculously easy to make, super pliable, easy to use, and so so tasty! The secret is marshmallows. So if you don't like marshmallows or powdered sugar, I guess you can go now (and really, why are you here in the first place?), but if you are totally into marshmallows try this. Oh, and P.S.—layer this on TOP of a smooth smear of buttercream for the best of both worlds!

• •

8 cups mini marshmallows

¼ cup water

2 pounds powdered sugar (about 8 cups)

¼ cup vegetable shortening, plus more for your hands

1. In a large, microwave-safe bowl, combine the marshmallows and water. Microwave for 1 minute. Remove the bowl from the microwave and stir. The marshmallows will begin to puff and melt. Return the bowl to the microwave and continue microwaving in 30-second intervals, stirring after each until mostly smooth.

2. Remove the bowl from the microwave and stir in half of the powdered sugar until combined.

3. Spread the vegetable shortening on a clean counter or work surface. Pour the remaining powdered sugar out onto the greased surface and then pour the marshmallow mixture out on top of the powdered sugar. Lightly grease your hands with more shortening to help with the stickiness and then knead all the powdered sugar into the marshmallow mixture until the fondant is a smooth, nonsticky ball.

4. Lightly coat the outside of the fondant with more shortening and wrap it airtight in plastic wrap.

5. Allow the fondant to rest for 30 minutes before using. Or, if not using right away, place the wrapped fondant into a large zip-top bag, squeezing any excess air out, and store at room temperature for up to 1 month.

Tips: To cover a layer cake in fondant: First bake your layers, then fill and frost the top and sides with a thin layer of frosting. On a work surface dusted with powdered sugar, unwrap the fondant. Coat a rolling pin with powdered sugar as well and roll the fondant out until it's ⅛ inch thick and big enough to cover the cake. Measure out the cake that you are covering in diameter and height, and add 2 inches to that measurement. It's always better to have extra fondant at the edges than not enough, so you can trim the edges for an even finish.

To cover cookies in fondant, such as my Classic Cut-Out Sugar Cookies (page 6): Roll out the fondant as described above. Use the same cookie cutter you used for the cookie to cut the perfect fondant shape. Brush the cookie lightly with corn syrup to work like glue and place the cut fondant on top of the cookie, pressing evenly and lightly to adhere the fondant to the corn syrup.

Pretzel Frosting

✦ *Makes 2 cups* ✦

*T*his might seem a little crazy. Pretzel frosting? I know, so weird, Shelly. But think about it . . . salty pretzel crumbs folded into a sweet buttery frosting . . . see? You're back on board, right? This creamy buttercream mash-up is the perfect filling for a chocolate cake, a great topper for a batch of brownies, or even a simple fruit dip to blow your friends' minds! Yep, leave it to me to take fruit dip downtown. The awesome thing about this frosting, too, is that if pretzels aren't your thing, you can grind up graham crackers or crispy chocolate chip cookies instead! It's like a frosting mix and match. Love it!

. . . .

1 cup (2 sticks) salted butter, at room temperature

3 cups powdered sugar

1 teaspoon vanilla extract

3 tablespoons whole milk or heavy cream

¾ cup finely ground pretzels

1. In the bowl of a stand mixer fitted with the paddle attachment, mix the butter on medium speed until smooth. Turn the speed to low and add the powdered sugar, vanilla, and milk, mixing until combined. Turn the speed back up to medium and mix until smooth and creamy, scraping the sides of the bowl as necessary.

2. Add the pretzel crumbs and mix until incorporated and smooth.

Store airtight at room temperature for up to 2 days, or refrigerated for up to 5 days. Allow the refrigerated frosting to come to room temperature before using.

Pie

Life's better in a crust.

Okay, so, pie. I get it. Pie is a whole thing in this world. My mom was a pretty clutch pie maker (baker). And my dad is a VERY clutch pie consumer. Unfortunately the pie gene didn't trickle down to me, on either the maker (baker) or consumer fronts. But I do realize that any baker worth their salt needs to know pie. So I learned. And I'll tell you, while fruit pies aren't my main squeeze, I do love pie crust filled with chocolate and all sorts of other nonfruit bits. But for the sake of my dad I included a fruit pie in this chapter. An apple one. Daughter of the Year Award, over here.

Epic Chocolate Pudding Pie

❖ *Serves 8–10* ❖

*T*his is my favorite pie that I make. There is just something about the creamy, rich, super-chocolaty filling that makes me savor every bite. The first time I made the thick, homemade chocolate pudding I knew my pie game had just reached the next level. Pairing the deep chocolate with a light whipped cream and a buttery crust turns every "I'll just have one bite" into "Hey, got any more of that pie?" I ain't mad about it.

• •

1 disc of All-Butter Pie Dough (page 20), chilled

FILLING:

2½ cups half-and-half

4 egg yolks

¾ cup granulated sugar

¼ cup cornstarch

¼ teaspoon kosher salt

1 tablespoon vanilla extract

2 tablespoons salted butter, cubed

3 ounces unsweetened chocolate, chopped

TOPPING:

1 cup cold heavy cream

2 tablespoons powdered sugar

1. Roll out the chilled pie dough into a 13-inch round, fit into a 9-inch pie plate, and prebake as directed on page 20. Let cool.

2. *For the filling:* In a medium bowl, whisk together the half-and-half and egg yolks. Set aside.

3. In a medium saucepan, whisk together the granulated sugar, cornstarch, and salt over medium heat for 1 minute. Immediately pour the half-and-half mixture into the saucepan with the sugar mixture and continue whisking until the mixture comes to a boil.

4. Remove the pan from the heat and quickly whisk in the vanilla, butter, and chocolate, stirring until the mixture is smooth.

5. Spread the chocolate pudding into the prebaked pie crust. Cover the pie and chill for at least 3 hours.

6. *For the topping:* Just before serving, combine the cream and powdered sugar in the bowl of a stand mixer fitted with the whisk attachment. Beat the cream on high speed until stiff peaks form. Spread the whipped cream over the pie.

7. Slice and serve.

Store airtight in the refrigerator for up to 3 days.

Over-the-Top Peanut Butter Cup Ice Cream Pie

❖ Serves 10–12 ❖

*O*h, this pie. Ohhhh. This pie. I ask you, urge you, nay, beseech you—make this. It's remarkably easy, super creamy, ribboned with peanut butter, and loaded with peanut butter cups, all on top of a peanut butter sandwich cookie crust. Also, let me mention the ice cream filling for this pie. My husband is a HUGE Klondike ice cream bar fan. He is obsessed with the ice cream, says it's the smoothest, creamiest one out there. So I learned a trick online a few years ago about mixing vanilla ice cream with Cool Whip to create an ultra creamy ice cream. Well, it works for sure. So this pie is filled with all the peanut butter goodness AND a super creamy vanilla ice cream. I also recommend going the extra mile and topping it with a little whipped cream and some hot fudge! There isn't much not to love.

. . . .

24 peanut butter sandwich cookies (such as Nutter Butter), finely crushed

5 tablespoons salted butter, melted

3 cups vanilla ice cream

2 cups Cool Whip, thawed

1 cup creamy peanut butter

14 full-size Reese's peanut butter cups, coarsely chopped

1. In a large bowl, mix together the cookie crumbs and melted butter. Press the mixture firmly and evenly into the bottom and up the sides of a deep-dish pie plate or a 9-inch springform pan. Chill the crust in the freezer for 30 minutes.

2. At the same as you put the crust in the freezer, remove the ice cream and allow it to soften at room temperature until it's a stir-able consistency. You don't want it to be completely thawed.

3. In a large bowl, gently and evenly stir together the soft ice cream and the Cool Whip.

4. Spread this into the chilled crust.

5. Place the peanut butter in a medium microwave-safe bowl and heat for 30 seconds until it's smooth and pourable. Drizzle the peanut butter on top of the ice cream and swirl it into the ice cream using a butter knife.

6. Sprinkle the chopped peanut butter cups on top of the pie and press them lightly into the ice cream.

7. Cover the pie tightly with plastic wrap and then foil, and chill for at least 4 hours or overnight.

8. Ten minutes before serving, remove the pie from the freezer to make it easier to slice.

Store the pie airtight in the freezer for up to 1 month.

Tip: You can't substitute whipped cream for the Cool Whip in this recipe. The consistency doesn't work well when it's frozen.

Payday Pie

*T*his pie is all things delicious: creamy, crunchy, salty, and sweet. The cool, creamy peanut butter mousse filling is balanced with the salty peanuts. Add to all of this a buttery pie crust and caramel sauce and you have everything you could possibly want in life. It's named after the popular candy bar, which is one of my husband's favorites!

- -

CRUST:

1 disc of All-Butter Pie Dough (page 20), chilled

⅔ cup caramel sauce, store-bought or homemade (page 159)

⅓ cup chopped salted peanuts

FILLING:

2½ cups cold heavy cream

½ cup powdered sugar

8 ounces cream cheese, at room temperature

½ cup creamy peanut butter

Chopped peanuts and caramel sauce, for garnish (optional)

1. *For the crust:* Roll out the chilled pie dough to a 13-inch round, and fit it into a 9-inch pie plate, and prebake as directed on page 20. Let cool.

2. Pour the caramel sauce evenly over the bottom of the prebaked pie crust. Sprinkle the peanuts over the caramel. Refrigerate the crust while you make the filling.

3. *For the filling:* In the bowl of a stand mixer fitted with the whisk attachment, beat the cream and powdered sugar on high speed until stiff peaks form. Transfer the whipped cream to a medium bowl so you can continue using the stand mixer.

4. Switch to the paddle attachment on the mixer and mix the cream cheese and peanut butter on medium speed for 1 to 2 minutes or until smooth and combined, scraping the sides of the bowl as necessary.

5. Set aside 1 cup of the whipped cream for the topping and fold the rest of the whipped cream into the cream cheese mixture until evenly incorporated.

6. Remove the crust from the refrigerator and carefully spread the filling on top of the caramel and peanuts.

7. Spread the reserved 1 cup whipped cream on top. If desired, garnish with a drizzle of caramel and a sprinkling of peanuts.

8. Chill the pie for at least 2 hours before serving.

Store airtight in the refrigerator for up to 3 days.

Gooey Chocolate Chip Pie

❧ Serves 10–12 ❧

This pie is my son David's favorite. He always requests it on Thanksgiving and even tried to learn to make it once. Unfortunately he tried to add nuts to the pie and ended up grabbing onion-seasoned nuts without realizing it. Turns out that onion nuts aren't a great addition to a chocolate chip pie, in case you were wondering! Needless to say I have omitted nuts from the recipe entirely, just so that never happens again. I've also banned my son from the kitchen during pie-making time. Obviously I'm kidding.

1 disc of All-Butter Pie Dough (page 20), chilled

1 cup (2 sticks) salted butter, at room temperature

1½ cups packed light brown sugar

2 large eggs

1 tablespoon vanilla extract

1 teaspoon baking soda

1 teaspoon kosher salt

2½ cups all-purpose flour

2½ cups semisweet chocolate chips

1. Preheat the oven to 350°F.

2. Roll out the chilled pie dough into a 13-inch round and fit it into a 9-inch deep-dish pie plate, trimming the extra and pinching the edges to form a rim. Set aside.

3. In the bowl of a stand mixer fitted with the paddle attachment, mix the butter and brown sugar on medium speed for 2 minutes until light and fluffy. Add the eggs and vanilla and continue mixing until smooth, scraping the sides of the bowl as necessary.

4. With the mixer still on medium, add the baking soda and salt and mix for 20 more seconds.

5. Turn the speed to low and add the flour, mixing until combined. Stir in the chocolate chips.

6. Spread the dough into the pie shell and bake for 25 to 30 minutes, until the edges are golden. If the center is a little undercooked, it will be fine!

7. Allow the pie to cool for at least 30 minutes before slicing.

Store airtight at room temperature for up to 3 days.

Tip: Serve warm with ice cream and hot fudge for a showstopping dessert!

Folded-Crust Apple Streusel Pie

✤ Serves 8–10 ✤

I can't make pie crusts pretty to save my life . . . and I have tried, trust me. So that's where this folded-crust pie comes in. Actually I think it's known on the street as a galette . . . but I prefer to call it like I see it, a folded crust. And what's extra-great about this pie is while it's all rustic and kind of messy, it's actually pretty fancy-looking . . . not sure how that happened. Drizzle it with caramel or top it with ice cream and you're set!

1 disc of All-Butter Pie Dough (page 20), chilled

FILLING:

4 large Granny Smith apples, peeled and thinly sliced

⅓ cup packed light brown sugar

2 tablespoons all-purpose flour

1 teaspoon ground cinnamon

STREUSEL:

4 tablespoons (½ stick) cold salted butter, cubed

½ cup packed light brown sugar

½ cup all-purpose flour

Caramel sauce, store-bought or homemade (page 159), for garnish (optional)

1. Preheat the oven to 375°F. Line a large baking sheet with parchment paper.

2. Roll out the chilled pie dough into a large round about 13 inches in diameter. It doesn't have to be exact. Transfer the dough carefully to the lined baking sheet.

3. *For the filling:* In a large bowl, combine the apples, brown sugar, flour, and cinnamon, stirring until evenly combined.

4. *For the streusel:* In another large bowl, mix the butter, brown sugar, and flour, cutting them together with a pastry cutter until the mixture resembles coarse sand. Form it into larger crumbs using your hands.

5. Place the apples in the center of the dough round, leaving a 2-inch border all around to fold over. Sprinkle the streusel mixture evenly on top of the apples. Fold the edges of the crust over the filling so it covers 1 to 2 inches of the apple mixture.

6. Bake the pie for 35 to 40 minutes, until the crust is golden brown and the center is bubbling.

7. Allow the pie to cool on the baking sheet and serve warm or at room temperature, garnished with caramel sauce if desired.

Store airtight at room temperature for up to 2 days.

Buttermint Pie

❖ Serves 10–12 ❖

A creamy, buttery mint is one of those candies I just can't turn down. Peppermint Patties, pastel mints, and of course Andes mints are all considered classics for good reason! There is a popular Italian restaurant chain that sends chocolate mints with the check. I have to admit it's brilliant—in no other restaurant am I so excited to pay the bill! Creating this pie was pretty simple, plus it's a no-bake recipe, which always makes me happy. You have a creamy, cool, minty filling on top of a crunchy, chocolaty crust. And of course I like to stick candies all over the top to make it extra yummy!

CRUST:

24 Oreo cookies, finely crushed

4 tablespoons (½ stick) butter, melted

FILLING:

8 ounces cream cheese, at room temperature

½ cup (1 stick) salted butter, at room temperature

2 cups powdered sugar

1 teaspoon peppermint extract

1 cup cold heavy cream

Whipped cream and chocolate mint candies, for garnish (optional)

1. *For the crust:* In a large bowl, combine the cookie crumbs and melted butter. Press the mixture firmly into a 9-inch pie plate. Chill the crust for at least 1 hour.

2. *For the filling:* In the bowl of a stand mixer fitted with the paddle attachment, mix the cream cheese and butter on medium speed until combined and smooth, scraping the sides of the bowl as necessary. Add the powdered sugar and peppermint extract and continue mixing until creamy. Transfer the cream cheese mixture to a bowl and set aside.

3. Wash the mixer bowl out and rinse with cold water and dry. Change to the whisk attachment and pour the heavy cream into the clean, cool bowl. Beat the cream until stiff peaks form.

4. Evenly fold the whipped cream into the cream cheese mixture and spread the filling into the chilled crust. Cover and refrigerate the pie for 4 hours or overnight.

5. Just before serving, garnish the pie with more whipped cream and chocolate mint candies, if desired.

Store airtight in the refrigerator for up to 3 days.

Salty Toffee-Banana Cream Pie

✦ Serves 10 ✦

I have never been a huge fan of plain bananas. My grandma used to make an amazing banana cream pie, which is what I based this recipe on. I adore banana bread, banana cupcakes, and really anything that has banana baked into it. But a banana on its own? Yeah, no. BUT I've found that when you disguise banana slices under a creamy mound of pudding and on top of a salty, buttery crust, even the biggest banana hater in your life will be convinced.

This pie is really easy to make, but there are a few steps to it with lots of chilling time needed, so make sure to read the instructions completely before getting started.

PUDDING BASE:

1 (3.4-ounce) box instant vanilla pudding

1 (14-ounce) can sweetened condensed milk

1¼ cups ice water

CRUST:

1¼ cups finely crushed pretzels

¼ cup granulated sugar

½ cup (1 stick) salted butter, melted

FILLING:

1 cup heavy cream

2 small bananas, thinly sliced

½ cup toffee bits (such as Heath Bits O' Brickle)

1. *For the pudding base:* In the bowl of a stand mixer fitted with the whisk attachment, combine the vanilla pudding, condensed milk, and ice water. Mix on medium speed for 2 minutes, until the mixture thickens slightly. Transfer to a bowl, cover, and chill for at least 4 hours.

2. *Meanwhile, for the crust:* While the pudding is chilling, preheat the oven to 350°F. Lightly coat a 9-inch pie plate with cooking spray.

3. In a medium bowl, evenly combine the pretzel crumbs, sugar, and melted butter. Firmly press the mixture into the bottom and up the sides of the pie plate.

4. Bake the crust for 10 minutes, or until lightly golden. Allow the crust to cool completely.

5. *For the filling:* When the pudding is chilled and the crust is completely cooled, in the bowl of a stand mixer fitted with the whisk attachment, beat the heavy cream on high speed until stiff peaks form. Fold the whipped cream into the chilled pudding until evenly incorporated.

6. Arrange the banana slices evenly over the cooled crust and sprinkle evenly with the toffee bits. Spread the filling mixture on top of the banana/toffee layer. Cover and chill the pie again for at least 2 hours.

Store airtight in the refrigerator for up to 3 days.

Tip: Use a food processor or blender to pulverize the pretzels for the crust.

Coconut Cream Pie

❧ Serves 8–10 ❧

I have to say that this is the only coconut cream pie recipe you will ever need. Each layer surpasses the next. It's baked in my all-butter pie crust, which is fantastic, but the filling is a creamy, rich custard speckled with sweetened coconut flakes. And the whipped cream might look harmless enough, but it's sweetened with cream of coconut (OMG), and finally there's epic coconut shortbread streusel on top, which brings it all together. The textures, the flavors . . . just everything together makes it pretty much unbeatable.

1 disc of All-Butter Pie Dough (page 20), chilled

CUSTARD FILLING:

2 cups half-and-half

5 egg yolks

½ cup granulated sugar

¼ cup cornstarch

¼ teaspoon kosher salt

2 tablespoons salted butter, cubed

1 teaspoon vanilla extract

1 cup sweetened flaked coconut

COCONUT STREUSEL:

¾ cup all-purpose flour

1 tablespoon granulated sugar

⅛ teaspoon kosher salt

¼ cup sweetened flaked coconut

4 tablespoons (½ stick) salted butter, melted

TOPPING:

1 cup cold heavy cream

2 tablespoons cream of coconut (such as Coco Lopez)

1. Roll out the chilled pie dough to a 13-inch round, fit it into a 9-inch pie plate, and prebake as directed on page 20. Let cool.

2. *For the custard filling:* In a medium bowl, whisk together the half-and-half and egg yolks. In a medium saucepan, whisk together the sugar, cornstarch, and salt. Slowly whisk in the yolk mixture until smooth. Whisking constantly over medium heat, bring the mixture to a boil, then immediately remove from the heat. Quickly add the cubed butter and vanilla and whisk until melted and incorporated. Fold in the coconut.

3. Cover this warm mixture with plastic wrap, allowing the wrap to touch the custard so a skin doesn't form. Allow to cool for 30 minutes at room temperature.

4. Spread the cooled custard into the prebaked pie crust, cover again with the plastic wrap touching the custard, and refrigerate for at least 1 hour.

5. *Meanwhile, for the coconut streusel:* Preheat the oven to 350°F. Line a baking sheet with parchment paper.

6. In the bowl of a stand mixer fitted with the paddle attachment, combine the flour, sugar, salt, and coconut on low speed. Add the melted butter and mix until it becomes a coarse crumble. Spread the mixture onto the prepared baking sheet and form the bits into larger crumbs using your hands. Bake for 15 to 20 minutes, until the streusel is golden brown. Remove from the oven and cool completely.

7. *For the topping:* Just before serving, in the bowl of a stand mixer fitted with the whisk attachment, mix the heavy cream and cream of coconut on high speed until stiff peaks form.

8. Remove the pie from the refrigerator and remove the plastic wrap. Spread the whipped cream on top of the custard layer and sprinkle as much coconut streusel on top of the whipped cream as desired.

Cover and refrigerate until ready to serve, up to 3 days.

Dessert Pizza

*C*alling this a pizza might be a bit misleading. But it is round, and there are toppings, and I do slice it into pizza-style wedges to serve it. So there. But it's actually a giant chocolate chip cookie topped with a creamy peanut butter frosting and a milk chocolate ganache garnished with pretzels and some flaked sea salt to make it look extra pretty. There isn't really a better party pie than this.

COOKIE CRUST:

1 cup (2 sticks) salted butter, at room temperature

1 cup packed light brown sugar

¼ cup granulated sugar

2 large eggs

2 teaspoons vanilla extract

1 teaspoon baking soda

1 teaspoon kosher salt

2¼ cups all-purpose flour

2 cups semisweet chocolate chips

PEANUT BUTTER TOPPING:

½ cup (1 stick) salted butter, at room temperature

½ cup creamy peanut butter

2 cups powdered sugar

1 tablespoon 2% or whole milk

MILK CHOCOLATE GANACHE:

2 cups milk chocolate chips

½ cup heavy cream

Pretzels and flaked sea salt, for garnish (optional)

1. *For the cookie crust:* Preheat the oven to 350°F. Coat a large (16-inch) round baking sheet or pizza pan with cooking spray.

2. In the bowl of a stand mixer fitted with the paddle attachment, mix the butter and both sugars on medium speed for 2 minutes. Add the eggs, vanilla, baking soda, and salt and continue mixing until the mixture is smooth, scraping the sides of the bowl as necessary.

3. Turn the speed to low and add the flour, mixing until just combined. Stir in the chocolate chips.

4. Press the dough evenly onto the prepared pan, leaving about a 1-inch border exposed, as the dough will expand when baking.

5. Bake the cookie for 15 to 20 minutes, until the edges are golden and the center is just set.

6. Allow to cool completely on the pan on a wire rack.

7. *For the peanut butter topping:* In the bowl of a stand mixer fitted with the paddle attachment, mix the butter and the peanut butter on medium speed for 1 to 2 minutes, until smooth and creamy.

8. Turn the speed to low and add the powdered sugar, mixing until combined. Add the milk and mix until creamy.

9. Spread the peanut butter onto the cooled cookie, leaving a border around the outside exposed (to look like the crust).

10. *For the milk chocolate ganache:* Place the milk chocolate in a heatproof medium bowl. In a small saucepan, heat the cream

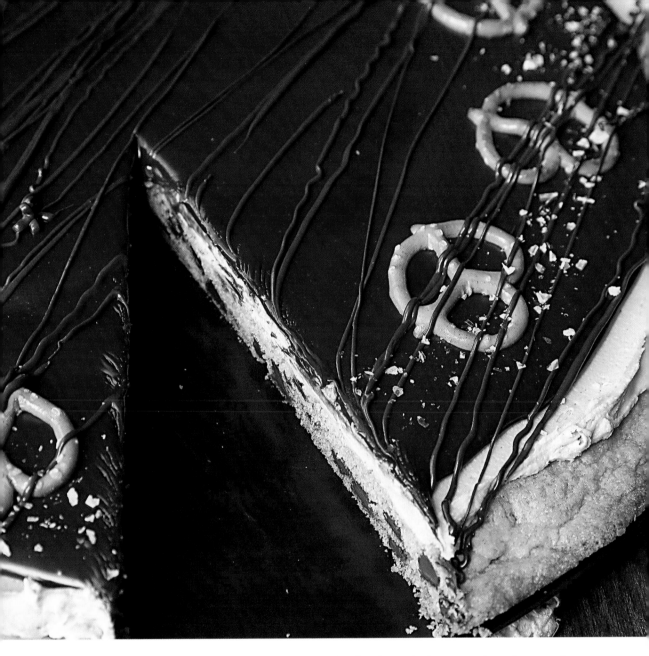

over medium heat until it starts to steam, stirring constantly. Alternatively, you can heat the cream in the microwave until very hot. Immediately pour the hot cream on top of the chocolate and stir until the chocolate is melted.

11. Spread the ganache on top of the peanut butter, using an offset spatula. If desired, garnish with pretzels and flaked sea salt.

Store airtight at room temperature for up to 3 days.

8

Party Snacks

It's not always about the cake.
I can't believe I just said that.

$\mathcal{I}$ like to think that all the recipes in this book
are party-worthy. Isn't that the baseline for a good
recipe? One that you would willingly share with
your nearest and dearest? But with that said, there
are definitely snacks or treats that can really make
a party better. I mean, yes, parties usually indicate
cake is involved, and I've got you covered there,
too, but what about all the time we spend hanging
around at get-togethers WAITING for the cake?
Let's make those minutes count, too. With party
snacks!

Salty Caramel Corn

❖ Makes 16 cups ❖

*T*his simple recipe is easily one of the most popular ones on my website, if not THE most popular. I get comments all the time from folks who make it, love it, and make it over and over again. It's the best caramel corn that I have ever had and I know you will love it, too. The recipe is simple, and the result is sweet and salty crispy popcorn that you won't be able to stop eating. I love to give it as gifts, or just sit down with a big bowl of it at night in front of a movie.

½ cup unpopped popcorn kernels

1 cup (2 sticks) salted butter

1 cup packed light brown sugar

⅓ cup light corn syrup

2 teaspoons kosher or sea salt

1. Preheat the oven to 300°F. Line a 15 x 18-inch rimmed baking sheet with parchment paper or a silicone baking mat.

2. Pop the popcorn kernels using an air popper into a large bowl. Set aside.

3. In a small saucepan, combine the butter, brown sugar, corn syrup, and 1 teaspoon salt. Bring to a boil over medium heat and allow it to boil for 4 minutes without stirring.

4. Drizzle the caramel mixture onto the popcorn and stir it to coat evenly.

5. Pour the coated popcorn into the prepared pan, sprinkle evenly with the remaining 1 teaspoon salt, and place the pan in the oven. Bake the popcorn for 30 minutes, stirring every 10 minutes.

6. Spread parchment paper onto your counter and, when the popcorn is done baking, pour it onto the prepared counter. Allow it to cool completely.

7. Sprinkle the popcorn with more salt if desired.

Store airtight at room temperature for up to 1 week.

Browned Butter Soft Pretzel Nuggets

❧ *Makes 6 dozen pretzel nuggets* ❧

*M*aking homemade pretzels is one of those tasks that I was always a little nervous to try. Any recipe that involves yeast gives me pause. BUT in the last few years I have found myself really getting into using yeast in dough. I am by no means an expert bread maker—yet—but I'm on my way to becoming one. And what I have found is it's best to start small. So when I began my yeast adventure I decided to scale pretzels down into bite-size pieces. Using browned butter in this recipe was a personal touch that I added to give the dough just a bit more depth. These never last long in my house!

4 tablespoons (½ stick) salted butter

1 cup warm water (not above 110°F)

1 (¼-ounce) envelope active dry yeast (2¼ teaspoons)

3 cups all-purpose flour

1 teaspoon kosher salt

2 tablespoons dark brown sugar

8 cups water

½ cup baking soda

Coarse or flaked sea salt or pretzel salt (optional)

1. In a medium saucepan, melt the butter over medium heat, then bring it to a boil. Once it starts boiling, swirl the pan constantly until the butter passes the foamy phase and becomes a deep amber color. Remove from the heat and allow the butter to cool slightly.

2. While the butter is cooling, pour the warm water into the bowl of a stand mixer fitted with the dough hook. Sprinkle the yeast into the water and allow the yeast to "bloom." This will take 7 to 9 minutes and the yeast will look slightly foamy.

3. Meanwhile, in a separate bowl, whisk together the flour, salt, and brown sugar.

4. When the yeast is ready, add the flour mixture and browned butter to the bowl with the yeast. Mix with the dough hook on medium speed for 5 minutes until the dough is elastic and smooth. If you find the dough too sticky, add additional flour 1 tablespoon at a time until the desired texture is reached.

5. Coat the inside of a large bowl with cooking spray and transfer the dough to the bowl. Cover with a clean kitchen towel and allow it to rise for 2 to 3 hours at room temperature until doubled in size. (Or place in the refrigerator and allow the dough to rise overnight, see Tip.)

6. When you're ready to make the pretzel bites, preheat the oven to 450°F. Line 2 baking sheets with parchment paper.

7. Remove the dough from the bowl and punch it down. Divide the dough into 8 equal portions and roll each portion into a 12-inch-long rope 1 inch in diameter. Cut each rope of dough crosswise into 2-inch lengths.

8. In a large saucepan, bring the water and baking soda to a boil. Working in batches of 10 to 12 pieces at a time, place the dough in the boiling water for 30 seconds. Remove with a slotted spoon and transfer to the prepared baking sheets. Immediately sprinkle the pieces liberally with salt (if using), as salt sticks best to the wet dough.

9. Bake the pretzels for 8 to 9 minutes, until golden brown.

10. Transfer to a wire rack to cool. Serve warm or at room temperature.

Store airtight at room temperature for up to 3 days.

Tips: If you plan on making the dough a day ahead and letting it rise in the refrigerator, you can coat a gallon-size zip-top bag with cooking spray and place the dough in the bag to help save fridge space.

You can serve these with mustard, melted cheese, or My Favorite Caramel Sauce (page 159).

Birthday Cake Trifle

*T*here are a few steps to this recipe, but don't let that intimidate you. Everything can be done in advance and it can be whipped up when you're ready! You can even make the whole trifle ahead and let it sit and marinate with all the over-the-top flavors. You have a homemade confetti cake and layers of rich custard, all topped with marshmallow buttercream. And of course a healthy dose of sprinkles!

· ·

Confetti Cake (page 118), baked and cooled

CUSTARD:

3 cups half-and-half

7 egg yolks

¾ cup granulated sugar

¼ cup plus 2 tablespoons cornstarch

½ teaspoon kosher salt

3 tablespoons cold salted butter, cubed

1½ teaspoons vanilla extract

MARSHMALLOW FROSTING:

1 cup (2 sticks) salted butter, at room temperature

1 cup Marshmallow Fluff

½ teaspoon vanilla extract

2 cups powdered sugar

1 cup rainbow sprinkles

1. *For the custard:* In a medium bowl, whisk together the half-and-half and egg yolks. In a medium saucepan, whisk together the sugar, cornstarch, and salt, then slowly whisk in the yolk mixture until smooth. Whisking constantly, bring the mixture to a boil over medium heat. Immediately remove from the heat and quickly whisk in the cubed butter and vanilla until melted and incorporated.

2. Cover this warm mixture with plastic wrap, allowing the wrap to touch the custard so a skin doesn't form. Allow to cool for 30 minutes at room temperature.

3. *Meanwhile, for the marshmallow frosting:* In the bowl of a stand mixer fitted with the paddle attachment, mix the butter and Marshmallow Fluff on medium speed for 1 minute until smooth. Add the vanilla and mix until incorporated.

4. Turn the speed to low and slowly add the powdered sugar. Once it's incorporated, turn the mixer back up to medium and mix for 1 more minute until smooth.

5. To assemble the trifle, cut the cake into 1½-inch cubes and divide into 3 equal portions.

6. In a large trifle dish, place one-third of the cake cubes on the bottom. Top the cake with half of the custard. Top the custard with ⅓ cup of the sprinkles. Repeat with another third of cake, the remaining custard, and ⅓ cup sprinkles. Top that with the remaining cake.

7. Spread as much of the marshmallow frosting as you would like on top of the last layer of cake and top with the remaining sprinkles.

Store refrigerated for up to 3 days. Allow the trifle to return to room temperature before serving.

Tip: You can also make these as 10 individual trifles in cups or mason jars by dividing everything into 10 equal portions and layering in the same order as for the large trifle.

Marble Sheet Cake

❖ Serves 15 ❖

*S*heet cakes are the best. They're pretty easy to make, they feed a crowd, and everyone likes them! I feel like I have come up with the perfect party sheet cake because, instead of having to choose between chocolate and vanilla, I've combined them together in a gorgeous marble cake that is simple to serve and even easier to eat!

CAKE:

1 cup (2 sticks) salted butter, at room temperature

1½ cups granulated sugar

2 large eggs

2 teaspoons vanilla extract

1 tablespoon baking powder

1 teaspoon kosher salt

2½ cups all-purpose flour

1 cup whole milk

¼ cup unsweetened cocoa powder

¼ cup hot water

FROSTING:

½ cup (1 stick) salted butter, cubed

¼ cup unsweetened cocoa powder

¼ cup plus 2 tablespoons whole milk

2 teaspoons vanilla extract

5 cups powdered sugar

1. *For the cake:* Preheat the oven to 325°F. Grease a 10 x 15-inch rimmed baking sheet with butter or shortening and flour lightly.

2. In the bowl of a stand mixer fitted with the paddle attachment, mix the butter and granulated sugar on medium speed for 2 minutes. Add the eggs, vanilla, baking powder, and salt and continue mixing on medium speed until smooth, scraping the sides of the bowl as necessary.

3. Turn the speed to low and add one-third of the flour, followed by half of the milk, beating after each addition. Repeat this step. End with a final addition of the flour and mix until just combined, scraping the sides so the mixture is smooth.

4. Measure out 1 cup of the batter and transfer to a medium bowl. Add the cocoa powder and hot water to the 1 cup batter and stir until evenly combined to make chocolate batter.

5. Spread the vanilla cake batter into the prepared pan. Drop the chocolate batter on top of the vanilla batter by the spoonful and, using a spoon or a knife, swirl the chocolate into the vanilla. Don't overmix, you want it only to be swirled, not mixed in.

6. Bake for 25 minutes, or until a toothpick inserted in the center comes out clean. Transfer the pan to a wire rack to cool slightly. You will want to frost your cake while it's still warm.

7. *Meanwhile, for the frosting:* In a large saucepan, combine the butter, cocoa powder, and milk and heat over medium heat until melted and smooth. Remove the pan from the heat and whisk in the vanilla and powdered sugar, mixing until smooth with no lumps.

8. Pour the frosting onto the warm cake and allow the cake to cool completely in the pan before serving.

Store airtight at room temperature for up to 3 days.

Buffalo Ranch Slow-Cooker Snack Mix

❖ Makes 13 cups ❖

I love salty snack mixes and if they're a tiny bit spicy . . . well . . . even better! My one complaint about snack mixes that you can buy premade is they never seem to have enough flavor for me. Also, I always end up combing through it for the things I want and leaving the sad snacks for the slowpokes. So, this snack mix is LOADED with flavor and *only* has things that I want in it! As an added bonus, I like to make it in the slow cooker. This is great for game nights, parties, or just to have while you're watching TV at night.

4 cups Rice Chex cereal

2 cups Wheat Chex cereal

4 cups small pretzel twists

2 cups Cheez-Its

1 cup salted peanuts

½ cup (1 stick) salted
   butter, melted

2 (1-ounce) envelopes
   ranch seasoning

1 tablespoon
   Worcestershire sauce

2 tablespoons hot sauce
   (such as Tabasco)

1. In a 6-quart slow cooker, mix the cereals, pretzels, Cheez-Its, and peanuts. In a small bowl, whisk together the melted butter, ranch seasoning, Worcestershire sauce, and hot sauce. Pour the mixture on top of the cereal mixture and stir to coat evenly.

2. Cover and cook on low for 3 hours, stirring every 30 minutes.

3. Line a counter with parchment paper and transfer the mix onto the lined counter. Allow it to cool completely. It will crisp up as it cools, so don't worry if it seems soft when you remove it from the slow cooker.

Store airtight at room temperature for up to 1 week.

Texas Sheet Cake in a Jar

Makes 9 (8-ounce) Mason jar-size trifles

Oh, my beloved Texas sheet cake. This recipe is one that I took from my grandma's recipe box, and I am sure you have a version of it at your house. I turned it into individual cake jars, because, heck, those little guys are freakin' adorable and perfect for parties. I have to say, it's one of the best ideas I've had in a long time. We all know, while Texas sheet cake is delicious, that it's really all about the poured chocolate frosting. And this recipe lets you have *lots* of frosting!

CAKE:

2 cups granulated sugar

2 cups all-purpose flour

½ teaspoon kosher salt

1 teaspoon baking soda

2 large eggs

1½ cups whole milk

1 tablespoon distilled white vinegar

2 teaspoons vanilla extract

½ cup (1 stick) salted butter

½ cup vegetable shortening

¼ cup unsweetened cocoa powder

FROSTING:

½ cup (1 stick) salted butter

¼ cup unsweetened cocoa powder

¼ cup plus 2 tablespoons whole milk

5 cups powdered sugar

2 teaspoons vanilla extract

1 cup chopped pecans

1. *For the cake:* Preheat the oven to 400°F. Generously coat a 10 x 15-inch rimmed baking sheet with cooking spray.

2. In a large bowl, whisk together the granulated sugar, flour, salt, and baking soda. Set aside.

3. In another bowl, whisk together the eggs, milk, vinegar, and vanilla. Set aside.

4. In a medium saucepan, melt the butter, shortening, and cocoa powder together over medium heat, whisking until completely melted and smooth.

5. Remove the chocolate mixture from the heat and pour into the flour mixture, stirring until just combined. Add the milk mixture and stir together until the batter is smooth and there are no more lumps.

6. Pour the batter into the prepared pan. Bake for 20 minutes, or until a toothpick inserted in the center of the cake comes out clean. Allow the cake to cool completely in the pan.

7. *For the frosting:* In a medium saucepan, combine the butter, cocoa powder, and milk and bring just to a boil over medium heat. Immediately remove the pan from the heat and whisk in the powdered sugar and vanilla until there are no lumps.

8. To assemble the cakes, use an 8-ounce Mason jar as a "cookie cutter." Flip the jar upside down and use the rim of the jar to cut the cake into rounds (this way the cake rounds will fit perfectly into the jars). As you will need to cut a total of 27 cake rounds, you need to leave as little excess cake as possible.

9. Place one cake round into the bottom of each jar. Top the cake with 2 tablespoons of chocolate frosting. Top the icing with a generous teaspoon of pecans. Repeat the process 2 more times so you end up with 3 layers per jar.

Cover the jars and store at room temperature for up to 3 days.

Snacking Granola

❧ Makes 10 cups ❧

*J*t might be shocking, but granola is one of my favorite snacks. Especially homemade granola. And I have to tell you, my recipe might be the best in all the land. I know that sounds like a fairly bold statement, considering that there are entire companies out there devoted solely to making granola. Well, sorry, granola companies, I've got your number. This recipe is remarkably easy, but there are a few tricks to making it perfect. Leaving it in the oven for hours after it's baked helps it stick together and form the yummy clusters, which we all know are the best part. I also add some crushed cornflakes to up the crunch factor! Beyond that you can switch up the add-ins and make it your own.

. . . .

5 cups old-fashioned rolled oats

1 cup raisins

2 cups sweetened flaked coconut

4 cups cornflakes, coarsely crushed

1 teaspoon kosher salt

1 cup whole salted cashews or any kind of nut

½ cup (1 stick) salted butter, melted

¾ cup packed light brown sugar

½ cup honey

1 large egg white, beaten

1 cup white chocolate chips

1. Preheat the oven to 300°F. Line your largest rimmed baking sheet with parchment paper. (I like to use my half-sheet cake pan, which is 12 x 18 inches.)

2. In a large bowl, mix together the oats, raisins, coconut, cornflakes, salt, and cashews.

3. In a medium bowl, mix together the butter, brown sugar, and honey. Pour over the oat mixture, stirring until evenly coated. Stir in the beaten egg white until evenly combined.

4. Spread the mixture onto the prepared baking sheet. Bake for 20 minutes without stirring and turn the oven off without opening the oven door. Allow the granola to remain in the oven until it's completely cooled, or up to overnight.

5. Remove the pan from the oven and sprinkle the white chocolate chips on top and break it into clusters.

Store airtight at room temperature for up to 1 week.

part two

DID YOU SAVE ROOM FOR DINNER?

Okay, so here we go. The world tells me we can't survive on only sweet treats. I guess the world can be right this once.

But since we're doing dinner here, we're going to do it my way! These are recipes that I make in my kitchen, serve to my family and friends, and enjoy on the reg. This is everyday food that I think is interesting but not complicated. I have so many cookbooks that are beautiful, and the recipes are unique and gorgeous and special, but they aren't things I would ever actually make on a busy, random Wednesday night. And my life is basically one giant series of busy, random Wednesday nights.

So, my approach to dinner in this book is to serve up recipes and ideas that you will actually make. And then make again, which we all know is the true test.

Pizza and Pasta

Let's carb up!

$\mathcal{J}$f you have kids under the age of 18 in your house, I am sure that pizza and pasta are staples in your weekly meal rotation. They always were in my house, growing up. We had Pizza Fridays and Spaghetti Wednesdays, and that's just the way it always was. Besides generally being easy meals to throw together, they usually run on the inexpensive side to make, and a lot of the time you have most of the ingredients in your pantry already. This chapter is all about taking your pizza and pasta game up a level.

Pizza Dough

✣ Makes 3 (15-ounce) portions ✣

We are a pizza family. A few years back my husband decided that we needed a wood-burning, brick pizza oven in our backyard. I know this sounds very, very fancy. Trust me, it isn't. My husband is a pretty handy guy. He is also a pretty crazy guy. He regularly finds new hobbies and hits them hard. In the years we've been together he has been (among other things) a car remodeler, a wine maker, a beer maker, a grill master, a hunter, a gun enthusiast, and an Amazon kingpin reviewer. Well, it turns out the summer of 2012 was the year of My Husband, The Pizza Maker. He researched pizza ovens for a long while prior to getting going with it (I am sure a lot longer than I even know). And then one day he told me he was running out. I didn't think much of it, until he came home with a ton or two of brick. So it began. Anyhow, after a lot of blood, sweat, and tears, we are now the owners of a giant pizza oven in our backyard that my mother-in-law likes to call the crematorium. Sounds delicious, doesn't it?

Obviously when we get the brick oven going we can make some pretty epic pies. But not every day is conducive to cranking it up. Which brings me to today. We make our own dough—don't be scared, it's easy—and I whip up a pizza indoors, my favorite method being my cast-iron skillet. It's SUPER easy, my kids love it, and once you have the dough made you can have a thick and delicious pizza in under 30 minutes. Love it. Sorry, honey.

. . . .

1 (¼-ounce) envelope active dry yeast (2¼ teaspoons)

1 cup warm water (not above 110°F)

1¼ cups ice water

1 teaspoon granulated sugar

1½ tablespoons kosher salt

2 tablespoons olive oil

5½ cups bread flour or all-purpose flour, plus more for kneading

1. In a small bowl, combine the yeast and lukewarm water and stir gently. Allow the yeast to dissolve for 5 minutes.

2. In another small bowl, combine the cold water, sugar, salt, and olive oil, stirring to dissolve the salt and sugar.

3. Place all the flour in the bowl of a stand mixer fitted with the dough hook. Add the yeast mixture and cold water mixture and mix on low speed for 7 minutes, until the dough forms a nonsticky ball. The dough might crawl up the side of the bowl, and if this happens just turn the mixer off and push the dough back down and start it up again.

4. Lightly flour a clean work surface. Transfer the dough to the floured surface and knead with your hands for 2 minutes until it forms a smooth ball. If the dough is sticky at all, add ¼ cup more flour at a time until it's smooth to the touch.

5. Divide the dough into 3 equal portions, weighing 15 ounces each. Form each portion into a ball, pinching the ends together.

6. Lightly coat the insides of 3 gallon-size zip-top bags with cooking spray. Place each dough ball into its own bag, removing as much excess air as possible. Place the dough in the refrigerator for at least 10 hours. The dough will double in size.

7. When you're ready to use the dough, remove it from the bag, punch it down, and allow it to come up to room temperature before you try stretching it.

Use the dough within 2 days, or freeze the risen dough for up to 1 month.

Tip: Using bread flour in this recipe will give you a crispier crust, while all-purpose flour will give you a chewier crust.

Monte Cristo Pizza

✤ Serves 4 ✤

I have been a huge fan of the Monte Cristo sandwich since I can remember. There was a chain restaurant near where I grew up called Bennigan's that had the most amazing Monte Cristo. If you are unfamiliar with the sandwich, it's ham and Gruyère cheese on bread, dipped in an egg batter and fried, generally dusted with powdered sugar and served with raspberry preserves. Might sound a little bit out there, but it's ridiculously good. Well, I decided to transform the Monte Cristo into a puff pastry "pizza," and I'm not ashamed to tell you it turned out pretty much perfecto!

. . . .

1 sheet frozen puff pastry, thawed according to package directions

4 ounces cream cheese, at room temperature

2 cups grated Gruyère cheese, divided

1 teaspoon dried parsley

Salt and pepper

6 ounces sliced deli ham, cut into thin strips

¼ cup raspberry preserves (optional)

1. Preheat the oven to 400°F. Line a baking sheet with parchment paper.

2. On a lightly floured surface, halve the sheet of puff pastry lengthwise. Using a fork, poke holes randomly in both halves. Bake these for 10 minutes, until the pastry is puffed and golden.

3. While the pastry is baking, in a medium bowl, combine the cream cheese, 1 cup of the Gruyère, the parsley, and the salt and pepper to taste. Set aside.

4. Remove the pastry from the oven, but leave the oven on and reduce the temperature to 350°F.

5. Allow the puff pastries to cool for 5 minutes, then, dividing evenly, carefully spread the cream cheese mixture onto each half, leaving a ½-inch border around the edges.

6. Top each half with ham and then sprinkle the remaining 1 cup Gruyère on top of the pizzas.

7. Return the baking sheet to the oven and bake for 20 minutes, or until the cheese is melted.

8. Remove from the oven and allow to cool for 5 minutes.

9. If desired, heat the raspberry preserves in the microwave for 20 to 30 seconds and drizzle on top of the pizza.

10. Serve hot.

Perfect Stovetop Mac and Cheese

⁘ Serves 4 ⁘

*M*ac and cheese is probably my favorite meal of all time. I grew up on the Kraft blue box stuff, and I have to say that there is still something very comforting and nostalgic about that boxed version. But as I've gotten older I have learned the value of cooking from scratch, and most of the time it ends up being just as easy as using ready mixes—not to mention a whole lot tastier. That's the case with this mac and cheese. It's ULTRA creamy, reminiscent of the popular Velveeta shells and cheese (without the Velveeta), and it can be made in about 20 minutes!

- -

1 pound medium pasta shells

2 cups grated mild cheddar cheese

1 cup grated sharp cheddar cheese

1¼ cups evaporated milk

2 large eggs

½ teaspoon kosher salt

1. Cook the pasta according to the package directions. Before draining, measure out and set aside about 1 cup of the pasta water.

2. Meanwhile, in a large pot or Dutch oven, whisk together both cheeses, the evaporated milk, eggs, and salt and cook over medium heat, stirring constantly, until the cheese is melted and the mixture is smooth.

3. Drain the pasta, add to the cheese mixture, and stir to coat the pasta completely. Add the reserved pasta water, 1 tablespoon at a time, until you reach the sauce consistency you desire. I usually end up using 3 to 4 tablespoons of pasta water.

4. Serve immediately.

Spicy Thai Noodles

*S*picy Asian noodles are one of those foods I could eat every day. Add some grilled shrimp or chicken and you have a hearty meal, or eat them plain for a simple dinner or lunch. AND you can eat these guys warm or cold, which I love. Grabbing a big bowl of noodles directly out of the fridge and digging in with a fork is my personal favorite. Keepin' it classy, folks! You can make these spicier if you're feeling daring, or milder if your kids are picky about spices. This is easy food at its finest.

½ cup vegetable or canola oil

2 tablespoons sesame oil

1 tablespoon rice vinegar

1 tablespoon lime juice

2 teaspoons crushed red pepper

1 clove garlic, minced

¼ cup less sodium soy sauce

¼ cup honey

1 pound spaghetti

½ cup chopped salted peanuts

2 medium carrots, grated

1 cup chopped cilantro

½ cup thinly sliced English cucumber

1. In a medium bowl, whisk together both oils, the vinegar, lime juice, red pepper flakes, garlic, soy sauce, and honey. Set aside.

2. Cook the pasta according to the package directions.

3. Drain the pasta and place in a large serving bowl. Pour the reserved dressing on top of the noodles and toss to coat. Add the peanuts, carrots, cilantro, and cucumber and stir to combine.

4. Serve warm or cold.

King Ranch Mac and Cheese

❖ Serves 6 ❖

My friend Kristan gave me the idea for this recipe. We were talking one day about ideas for dinners and she told me she made "King Ranch Mac and Cheese" a lot for freezer meals or to give to people to heat up. I love any version of cheesy pasta out there, so I gave her recipe a try. Over the past few years I have made this pasta so many times I can't even count, and every time I've changed something here or there, finally creating this version of the pasta that we like so so much! Some of the best recipes come from friends!

. . . .

8 ounces cavatappi pasta

2 tablespoons salted butter

½ medium yellow onion, diced

½ medium green bell pepper, diced

½ medium red bell pepper, diced

2 cloves garlic, minced

1 (10-ounce) can diced tomatoes with green chilies

1 pound pasteurized prepared cheese product (such as Velveeta), cubed

½ cup sour cream

⅔ cup half-and-half

1½ teaspoons ground cumin

½ teaspoon cayenne pepper

4 cups cooked chicken (such as shredded rotisserie chicken)

1½ cups grated cheddar cheese

1. Preheat the oven to 400°F.

2. Cook the pasta according to the package directions and drain.

3. Meanwhile, heat a large skillet over medium heat. Melt the butter in the skillet and sauté the onion and bell peppers until soft, 7 to 8 minutes. Add the garlic and cook for 1 minute longer.

4. Add the diced tomatoes and cook until almost all of the liquid has evaporated, 3 to 4 minutes. Add the cubed cheese and stir constantly until the cheese is melted.

5. With the skillet still over medium heat, stir in the sour cream and half-and-half. Season with the cumin and cayenne pepper. Stir in the chicken.

6. In a 3-quart Dutch oven or baking dish, combine the chicken/cheese mixture with the cooked pasta evenly. Sprinkle with the grated cheddar and bake until the cheddar is melted and the mixture is bubbling, 5 to 10 minutes.

7. Serve hot.

Taco Pasta

❧ Serves 6 ❧

J have a kiddo who is taco-obsessed. I swear, you put taco seasoning in just about anything, and suddenly it becomes his latest favorite. So this recipe for taco pasta was 100 percent his idea. I helped him as he added a little bit of this and a little bit of that until we came up with a dish he is super proud of. The taco lover in your life will definitely thank you for this one!

1 pound rotini pasta

1 pound lean ground beef

1 (28-ounce) can crushed tomatoes

¾ cup salsa

1 (1.25-ounce) envelope taco seasoning (*see DIY option*)

2 teaspoons ground cumin

1 tablespoon chili powder

½ teaspoon cayenne pepper

1 (14-ounce) can whole kernel corn, drained

1 (14-ounce) can black beans, drained and rinsed

1½ cups grated cheddar cheese

¼ cup chopped cilantro, for garnish

1. Preheat the oven to 400°F.

2. Cook the pasta according to the package directions and drain.

3. Meanwhile, in a 10-inch ovenproof skillet, brown the ground beef over medium-high heat. Drain off any excess fat from the skillet.

4. Reduce the heat to medium and add the crushed tomatoes, salsa, taco seasoning, cumin, chili powder, and cayenne pepper and stir to combine. Add the corn and black beans and stir again to evenly incorporate the ingredients.

5. Add the drained pasta carefully to the meat mixture and stir to evenly combine.

6. Top the pasta mixture with the grated cheddar and bake until the cheese is melted, 10 to 15 minutes.

7. Garnish with cilantro and serve hot.

{ DIY OPTION! }
Taco Seasoning
❧ Makes ⅓ cup ❧

There is no reason that you have to continue buying those little packets of taco seasoning. Please believe! Making it on your own creates a more flavorful, fresher-tasting seasoning mixture, and it also allows you to control how much salt you are consuming. It's all about control, folks. Two tablespoons of homemade taco mix seasons 1 pound of ground meat perfectly. Double or even triple this recipe if you make tacos a lot!

· ·

2 tablespoons ground cumin

1 tablespoon chili powder

2 teaspoons kosher salt

1 teaspoon garlic powder

1 teaspoon onion powder

1 teaspoon smoked paprika

¾ teaspoon white pepper

½ teaspoon cayenne pepper

Mix all the ingredients together evenly.

Store airtight for up to 6 months.

Sunday Sauce and
Spicy Cheesy Meatballs

❖ Serves 12 ❖

*T*his sauce is a family tradition. I almost feel guilty sharing it here with you . . . but you're kind of like my extended family, so it's all good. This sauce is a fresh take on the recipe that my mother-in-law has made for years. My husband taught me how to make it when we started dating, and since then I have taken over the Sunday Sauce–making in our house. While I can't say that we make it every Sunday, we do make it very often. The sauce simmers on the stovetop all day long, so your house will smell fantastic! The recipe makes a large pot of sauce, enough for 3 pounds of pasta, so invite your friends over and make it a tradition in your house as well!

SUNDAY SAUCE:

2 tablespoons olive oil

1 pound sweet Italian sausage links, halved

½ cup diced onion

4 cloves garlic, minced

¼ cup tomato paste

4 (28-ounce) cans crushed tomatoes

½ cup red wine (optional)

1 teaspoon granulated sugar

1½ teaspoons dried basil

1½ teaspoons dried oregano

½ to 1 teaspoon crushed red pepper (to taste)

1 teaspoon kosher salt

MEATBALLS:

2 pounds meatloaf mix (50/20/30 ground beef/veal/pork)

2 large eggs

1. *For the Sunday Sauce:* In a large saucepan or Dutch oven, heat the olive oil over medium-high heat. Add the Italian sausage and cook until browned. Remove the sausage from the pot and set aside.

2. Reduce the heat to medium, add the onion to the pot, and cook until soft, about 5 minutes. Add the garlic and cook for 2 minutes, stirring often. Add the tomato paste and stir to coat the onion and garlic.

3. Return the sausage to the pot, then add the crushed tomatoes, wine (if using), sugar, basil, oregano, red pepper flakes, and salt. Stir the mixture to combine and bring it to a low simmer. Reduce the heat to low and cook the sauce uncovered for at least 2 hours before you add the meatballs, stirring occasionally. The longer the sauce cooks, the better.

4. *For the meatballs:* When the sauce has been cooking for 2 hours, make your meatballs. In a large bowl, combine the meatloaf mix, eggs, ricotta, breadcrumbs, parsley, red pepper flakes, and Parmesan. You want all the ingredients to be evenly incorporated, but try not to overwork the meat, which will result in dense meatballs. Form the mixture into 1½-inch balls.

5. In a large skillet, heat the oil over medium heat. The oil is ready when the tip of a wooden spoon handle inserted in the oil forms tiny bubbles.

½ cup whole-milk ricotta cheese

½ cup Italian seasoned dried breadcrumbs

1 tablespoon dried parsley

1½ teaspoons crushed red pepper

1 cup freshly grated Parmesan cheese

½ cup vegetable or light olive oil, for frying

6. Working in batches, add the meatballs to the hot oil and cook until golden brown on all sides, 4 to 5 minutes per batch. Using a slotted spoon, transfer the meatballs to the sauce.

7. Cook the meatballs in the sauce for at least 1 hour or up to 2 hours.

8. Serve over pasta.

Store airtight in the refrigerator for up to 5 days, or in the freezer for up to 1 month. If freezing, separate the meatballs and sausage from the sauce.

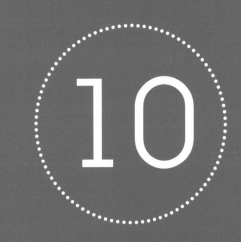

10

Salads and Sammies

Lighter food that will put some meat on your bones.

$\mathcal{I}$f you're looking for a meal that's a little less meal-ish, this chapter is for you. I can't really say that the recipes are lighter on calories, because these ARE actual dinners that will satisfy even the largest appetites. Salads happen to be one of my favorite things to eat. Oh, I don't mean garden salads, silly . . . I mean a whole big salad with lots of add-ins and flavors. There is a meal in this chapter for everyone, except your vegan friends. Sorry, guys.

Asian Lettuce Wrap
Chicken Chopped Salad

⁂ Serves 4 ⁂

*A*sian lettuce wraps are one of my favorite appetizers to order when we go out to eat. The only thing is, I am a messy eater and always end up with a fork in one hand, eating the "wraps" like a salad. So clearly that's where I got the idea for this salad. It's basically a deconstructed lettuce wrap, and I have to say, it makes way more sense than in wrap form—to me, at least.

SALAD DRESSING:

3 tablespoons rice vinegar

3 tablespoons vegetable oil

1 teaspoon sesame oil

1 teaspoon honey

1 teaspoon grated fresh ginger

1 clove garlic, minced

Salt and pepper

CHICKEN:

¼ cup hoisin sauce

1 tablespoon rice vinegar

2 teaspoons Sriracha sauce

2 tablespoons less sodium soy
   sauce

1 teaspoon grated fresh ginger

1 teaspoon sesame oil

1 tablespoon olive oil

1 pound ground chicken

8 ounces canned water chestnuts,
   diced

⅓ cup chopped unsalted cashews

2 scallions, thinly sliced

SALAD:

1 head Boston or Bibb lettuce,
   chopped

1 romaine lettuce heart, chopped

2 carrots, grated

1. *For the dressing:* In a small bowl, whisk together the vinegar, oils, honey, ginger, garlic, and salt and pepper to taste. Set the dressing aside.

2. *For the chicken:* In a medium bowl, whisk together the hoisin, vinegar, Sriracha, soy sauce, ginger, and sesame oil. Set aside.

3. In a medium skillet, heat the olive oil over medium-high heat. Add the chicken and cook until browned and cooked through, 8 to 10 minutes. Drain any excess fat or liquid.

4. Add the water chestnuts and cashews to the pan. Pour the reserved hoisin mixture on top and cook for 1 to 2 minutes to heat through. Stir in the scallions. Remove from the heat and set aside.

5. *For the salad:* In a large salad bowl, combine both of the lettuces and the carrots. Toss the salad with the dressing and top with the chicken mixture.

6. Serve immediately.

Tip: Alternatively, you can assemble 4 salads in separate bowls for individual portions.

BLT Panzanella Salad

$\mathcal{I}$ am basically obsessed with this salad. It's ridiculously simple, full of flavor, and HELLO . . . there's a pound of bacon in there. What's not to love? Panzanella salads are one of my all-time favorites: The pieces of toasty bread that soak up the dressing along with the crunchy lettuce make for the perfect bite. BLT sandwiches are a classic, and this salad takes all the elements of that and knocks it on its face. You guys will love this.

. . . .

DRESSING:

2 tablespoons red wine
   vinegar

1 tablespoon spicy brown
   mustard

2 tablespoons olive oil

1 tablespoon water

Salt and pepper

SALAD:

½ French baguette, halved
   lengthwise

2 tablespoons olive oil

Salt and pepper

2 romaine lettuce hearts,
   chopped

1 pint grape tomatoes,
   halved

1 pound bacon, cooked
   until crisp and chopped
   into bite-size pieces

1. Preheat the oven to 400°F.

2. *For the dressing:* In a small bowl, whisk together the vinegar, mustard, oil, water, and salt and pepper to taste. Set aside.

3. *For the salad:* Drizzle the cut side of the baguette with the olive oil and season with salt and pepper. Place on a baking sheet and lightly toast in the oven for 4 to 5 minutes. When cool enough to handle, cut into cubes.

4. Meanwhile, in a large salad bowl, combine the lettuce, tomatoes, and bacon. Add the dressing and toss.

5. Add the toasted bread cubes and toss into the salad evenly.

6. Serve immediately.

Frito Pie Sloppy Joes

❖ Serves 8 ❖

*G*rowing up in the South, Frito Pie was standard game-day food. So imagine my dismay when I moved up to New Jersey and no one seemed to know what a Frito Pie was! When I first mentioned the simple dinner (which is typically chili served on top of a big handful of Fritos), I was met with confused stares. I'm assuming they heard the word "pie" and thought it was a dessert. Anyhow, I decided to take this apparently confusing dish one step further and turn my Frito Pie into a sandwich. It's a sandwich you might need a fork to eat, but a sandwich, nonetheless.

2 tablespoons olive oil

1 small onion, diced

1 medium red bell pepper, diced

2 pounds lean ground beef

2 cloves garlic, minced

2 (15-ounce) cans tomato sauce

1 tablespoon Worcestershire sauce

1 tablespoon grill seasoning (*see DIY option*)

1 tablespoon red wine vinegar

1 teaspoon ground cumin

1 tablespoon chili powder

8 hamburger buns

2 cups grated cheddar cheese (optional)

Fritos, for topping the burgers

1. In a large skillet, heat the olive oil over medium heat. Add the onion and bell pepper and sauté until the onion begins to soften, about 5 minutes. Add the beef and garlic and continue cooking until the beef is cooked through, 8 to 9 minutes. Drain any excess fat from the pan.

2. With the pan still over medium heat, stir in the tomato sauce, Worcestershire sauce, grill seasoning, vinegar, cumin, and chili powder. Bring the mixture to a low boil, then reduce the heat to low and simmer for 10 minutes.

3. To assemble the sandwiches, top each bun with a scoop of the meat mixture, cheese (if using), and a handful of Fritos.

Grill Seasoning

❧ *Makes ⅓ cup* ❧

J adore grill seasoning. It has a little bit of everything in there and it's a great all-purpose ingredient that amps up the flavor of any food, from burgers and steaks to soups and sandwiches! It's a one-stop-shop seasoning.

2 tablespoons kosher salt

2 tablespoons coarsely ground black pepper

2 tablespoons garlic powder

1½ teaspoons onion powder

1½ teaspoons crushed red pepper

1 teaspoon smoked paprika

In a small bowl, mix together the salt, black pepper, garlic powder, onion powder, red pepper flakes, and smoked paprika.

Store airtight at room temperature for up to 6 months.

Chipotle-Lime Chicken Chopped Salad with Creamy Avocado Dressing

❧ Serves 4 ❧

$\mathcal{W}$hen we go out to eat I am pretty predictable. If there is any version of a Southwestern chicken salad on the menu, I will order it. Every. Dang. Time. I'm not quite sure what I love so much about Tex-Mex–type salads, but they own my order. Maybe it's because the lettuce is low man on the totem pole? These types of salads are generally filled up with loads of extras, including corn, beans, and tortillas chips. I mean, what's better than a salad with chips in it? Let me answer that for you: frosting . . . only frosting is better. And until the day I eat a frosting salad, this one will remain at the top of my list. The spicy chipotle and the bright lime complement each other perfectly, and the creamy avocado dressing is good enough to eat on its own! Let's do this!

MARINADE AND CHICKEN:

¼ cup lime juice

2 tablespoons sauce from canned chipotles in adobo

2 tablespoons olive oil

1 tablespoon honey

1 teaspoon ground coriander

2 cloves garlic, minced

1 pound boneless, skinless chicken breasts

CREAMY AVOCADO DRESSING:

1 avocado, halved and pitted

¼ cup canola oil

¼ cup water

2 tablespoons rice vinegar

1 tablespoon lime juice

1 clove garlic, minced

½ cup chopped cilantro

Salt and pepper

SALAD:

2 small (or 1 large) head of romaine lettuce, chopped

1 avocado, diced

1 cup canned whole kernel corn, drained

1 cup canned black beans, drained and rinsed

½ cup diced red bell pepper

1 cup coarsely crushed tortilla chips

Lime wedges, for garnish (optional)

1. *For the marinade and chicken:* In a bowl, mix together the lime juice, adobo sauce, olive oil, honey, coriander, and garlic. Place the chicken in a shallow bowl or large zip-top bag and pour the marinade over the chicken, stirring to coat. Allow the chicken to marinate for at least 4 hours.

2. *For the creamy avocado dressing:* Scrape the avocado into a blender or food processor. Add the canola oil, water, vinegar, lime juice, garlic, cilantro, and salt and pepper to taste. Pulse until completely smooth. The dressing should be on the thicker side, but if you feel like it is too thick, add a teaspoon of water at a time and mix until the desired consistency is reached.

3. *For the salad:* In a large bowl, combine the lettuce, avocado, corn, black beans, bell pepper, and tortilla chips. Wait to dress the salad until you're ready to serve it.

4. Preheat a grill to medium-high. Grill the chicken until cooked through, about 6 minutes on each side. Allow the chicken to sit for 5 to 10 minutes, then slice into strips.

5. Toss the salad with the dressing. Serve the chicken strips on a bed of salad. Garnish with lime wedges, if desired.

Thai Turkey Burgers with Spicy Asian Slaw

❧ Makes 9 (⅓-pound) burgers ❧

*I*n the summer we grill out a lot. So much so, actually, that we have more than the appropriate number of grills on our deck. My husband says they all serve their own purpose (of course). Getting creative with burgers has become a family event in my house—everyone has an idea! The great thing about a burger is it's a solid base for adding your favorite toppings and spices, which is where we got the idea for these Thai turkey burgers. And by adding slaw on top, you get a cool, spicy crunch that really makes it outstanding.

3 pounds ground turkey

1 cup panko breadcrumbs

¾ cup Thai sweet chili sauce

½ cup chopped cilantro

2 teaspoons kosher salt

9 hamburger buns

Spicy Asian Slaw (recipe follows)

1. Line a large baking sheet with parchment or wax paper. Set aside.

2. In a large bowl, mix together the turkey, panko, sweet chili sauce, cilantro, and salt until evenly incorporated. Form the meat mixture into patties that weigh ⅓ pound. You should get 9 burgers.

3. Place the burgers on the lined baking sheet and freeze for at least 1 hour, or until ready to use.

4. Preheat a grill to medium-high. Place the burgers on the hot grill and cook for 7 to 8 minutes, flipping once, until the burgers are cooked through and the internal temperature reads 165°F.

5. Serve the burgers on buns and topped with slaw.

SPICY ASIAN SLAW

❧ Makes 4 cups ❧

This can be made up to 1 day ahead.

DRESSING:
2 tablespoons soy sauce
2 tablespoons creamy peanut butter
1 tablespoon rice vinegar
1 tablespoon water
1 teaspoon sesame oil
1 clove garlic, minced
½ teaspoon crushed red pepper

SLAW:
3 cups shredded cabbage
1 cup grated carrots
½ cup chopped cilantro
⅓ cup finely chopped fresh (or canned crushed) pineapple
2 scallions, thinly sliced (optional)

1. *For the dressing:* In a medium bowl, whisk together the soy sauce, peanut butter, vinegar, water, sesame oil, garlic, and red pepper flakes.

2. *For the slaw:* In a large bowl, combine the cabbage, carrots, cilantro, pineapple, and scallions (if using).

3. Pour the dressing on top of the slaw and stir to coat evenly.

11

Family Favorites

*Meals my whole family
agrees on. In other words,
Miracle Food.*

$\mathscr{T}$he recipes in this chapter are meals my family can all agree on. I have four boys, so finding dinners that everyone loves is challenging. But I've found that taking a classic dish and morphing it into a meal that's creative and fun to eat is a great way not only to keep my family interested but also to keep me out of the weeknight dinner rut. I think some (or hopefully all) of these recipes will become favorites in your house as well!

Philly Cheesesteak–Stuffed Baked Potatoes

❖ Serves 6 ❖

*S*tuffed baked potatoes are a meal that I grew up on. In Houston, where I lived most of my childhood, there was a restaurant not too far from my house that served the HUGEST BBQ-stuffed potatoes. I am talking 9-inch potatoes overflowing with pulled pork dripping in BBQ sauce and topped with melted cheese, bacon, and maybe some sour cream and chives if you were feeling crazy. We ended up getting these monster BBQ potatoes once a week or so for dinner. When I moved to New Jersey, no one seemed to stuff their taters. It felt like a real tragedy at the time. (I know, I know—between this and the Frito Pie calamity, it's a miracle I didn't book the first flight I could find back to Texas!) Anyhow, I knew I wanted to include a spin on my beloved stuffed baked potatoes in this book. This version is the cream of the crop—the peppers get sweet as they cook and the provolone cheese sauce might be my new favorite food group!

6 russet (baking) potatoes

4 tablespoons olive oil

Salt and black pepper

2 green bell peppers, cut into thin strips

1 red bell pepper, cut into thin strips

1 medium yellow onion, thinly sliced

1½ teaspoons grill seasoning (*DIY option page 255*)

1 pound sliced deli roast beef, cut into strips

2 tablespoons butter

2 tablespoons all-purpose flour

2 cups whole milk, warmed

1 cup grated provolone cheese

½ cup freshly grated Parmesan cheese

1. Preheat the oven to 425°F. Line a baking sheet with foil.

2. Wash and scrub each potato well and pat dry. Place the potatoes on the lined baking sheet. Coat the potatoes with 2 tablespoons of the olive oil, sprinkle with salt and black pepper, and prick several times with a fork.

3. Bake the potatoes for 45 to 60 minutes, until soft and a fork can easily be inserted with no resistance.

4. When the potatoes are almost done baking, heat the remaining 2 tablespoons olive oil in a large skillet. Add the bell peppers and onion and cook until soft, 10 to 15 minutes. Sprinkle with the grill seasoning and add the sliced roast beef. Reduce the heat to low and cook until the roast beef is warm. Remove the skillet from the heat, cover, and set aside.

5. In a medium saucepan, melt the butter over medium heat. Whisk in the flour and cook for 1 minute. Slowly whisk in the warm milk, whisking constantly. Cook until thickened slightly, 4 to 5 minutes. Remove the saucepan from the heat and whisk in the provolone and Parmesan until melted and smooth.

6. To assemble the potatoes, split each potato lengthwise, and stuff the roast beef and pepper mixture in the middle of the potato. Top everything with the warm cheese sauce and serve hot.

Nacho Soup

✥ Serves 8 ✥

*N*achos might be the perfect food. You can top the salty tortilla chips with melty cheese and just about anything else and call it a meal. Getting creative with nachos is a favorite dinner event at my house! This soup takes all the flavors of a traditional nacho and turns it on its head. The soup is creamy and cheesy, loaded with all the elements of a perfect nacho, and then it's garnished with cheesy nacho chips. You'll need both a spoon and your fingers to eat this dinner mash-up!

1 pound lean ground beef or ground turkey

1 (1.25-ounce) envelope taco seasoning or 2 tablespoons homemade taco seasoning (page 239)

1 cup canned black beans, drained and rinsed

1 cup canned corn, drained

1 cup salsa

4 tablespoons (½ stick) salted butter

¼ cup all-purpose flour

3 cups chicken stock

3 cups whole milk

16 ounces cheddar cheese, grated

NACHO GARNISH:

4 cups tortilla chips

1½ cups grated cheddar cheese

1. In a large skillet, brown the ground beef over medium-high heat. Drain any excess fat.

2. Reduce the heat to low, sprinkle the taco seasoning onto the meat, and stir to combine. Stir in the black beans, corn, and salsa and continue cooking until combined and warm. Cover the skillet and remove from the heat.

3. In a 3- to 4-quart Dutch oven or saucepan, melt the butter over medium heat. Whisk in the flour and cook for 1 minute. Whisking constantly, pour the chicken stock into the pan slowly until combined and smooth. Continuing to whisk, slowly add the milk. Bring this mixture just to a boil, stirring constantly.

4. Reduce the heat to low and whisk in the cheddar, stirring until melted and smooth. Add the beef mixture to the soup, stirring until mixed. Cover the pot and keep warm while you make the nacho garnish.

5. *For the nacho garnish:* Preheat the oven to 400°F.

6. Spread the tortilla chips on a baking sheet and top with the cheddar. Bake for 5 minutes, or until the cheese is melted.

7. Serve the soup in bowls topped with the cheesy chips.

Chicken-Fried Steak
Meatballs and Gravy

❖ Serves 6 ❖

*C*hicken-fried steak is another staple of my Texan upbringing that hasn't quite solidified its deserved place on the tables of Northeasterners. I feel like I should have created a separate section in this book titled "Enlightening NJ: One Woman's Quest to Bring Southern Staples to the North." In any case, I ended up learning how to make my own at home and I'll tell ya, I feel like I have it nailed. My kids request it all the time, but it's one of those meals I try to limit to a few times a year. A light meal it isn't, so I came up with the idea for these chicken-fried steak meatballs which are far smaller in portion size than the standard, big-as-your-face chicken-fried steaks I grew up on. They make a great appetizer or meal and there's plenty to go around so everyone can try them. And just so you know, it's ALL about the gravy here, you guys.

- -

MEATBALLS:

2 pounds lean ground beef

2 teaspoons grill seasoning
   (*DIY option page 255*)

2 large eggs

½ cup dried breadcrumbs

2 cups all-purpose flour

1½ teaspoons kosher salt

1 teaspoon pepper

¾ cup whole milk

Vegetable oil, for frying

GRAVY:

⅓ cup all-purpose flour

3½ to 4 cups whole milk

Salt and pepper

1. *For the meatballs:* Preheat the oven to warm, or its lowest setting. Line a baking sheet with paper towels.

2. In a large bowl, combine the ground beef, grill seasoning, 1 of the eggs, and breadcrumbs until evenly incorporated. Form the mixture into 1-inch balls. Set aside.

3. In a shallow bowl, mix together the flour, salt, and pepper. In another shallow bowl, whisk together the milk and the remaining egg.

4. In a large skillet, add enough vegetable oil to cover the bottom of the pan (about ½ cup). Heat over medium heat.

5. While the oil is heating, start coating the meatballs. Dip each meatball into the flour mixture and coat, then into the egg mixture, and finally back into the flour mixture. Repeat this until all the meatballs are coated.

6. When the oil is hot, fry the meatballs in batches, taking care not to crowd the pan, until golden brown on each side. Transfer the first batches of meatballs to the lined baking sheet and place in the oven to keep warm while you fry the remaining meatballs. Add more oil to coat the pan in between batches, if necessary.

7. When all the meatballs are cooked and in the oven keeping warm, immediately prepare your gravy.

8. *For the gravy:* Measure out ⅓ cup of the frying oil from the meatballs and set aside. Discard any remaining oil. Without cleaning the skillet, return the reserved oil back to the hot pan, still over medium heat. Whisk the flour into the oil, stirring constantly. Cook the flour for 1 minute. Slowly whisk in 3½ cups of the milk, stirring constantly. Add salt and pepper to taste and cook until the gravy thickens. If the gravy gets too thick, add the remaining milk a little bit at a time until you reach the desired consistency.

9. Serve hot.

Tip: I like to serve the gravy in a bowl to dip the meatballs, but if dipping isn't your thing go ahead and smother the meatballs in the gravy!

Homemade Takeout: Cashew Chicken

❧ Serves 6 ❧

$\mathcal{M}$y husband and kids are huge fans of Chinese takeout. Of course everyone has their "usual" order, and mine is ALWAYS Cashew Chicken. The crunchy nuts and veggies mixed with the chicken and slightly spicy sauce just gets me every time. I knew creating a version at home would not only be tastier and fresher, but it would also be a little lighter on calories. Which means I can have an extra cookie after dinner!

SAUCE:

½ cup chicken stock

¼ cup less sodium soy sauce

2 tablespoons rice vinegar

2 tablespoons hoisin sauce

2 tablespoons honey

2 teaspoons Sriracha sauce

1½ teaspoons sesame oil

1½ teaspoons grated fresh ginger

½ to 1 teaspoon crushed red pepper (to taste)

2 tablespoons cornstarch

CHICKEN:

2 teaspoons canola oil

1½ pounds boneless, skinless chicken breasts, thinly sliced into 2-inch strips

Salt and pepper

2 medium carrots, julienned

8 ounces snow peas

1 clove garlic, minced

1 (8-ounce) can sliced water chestnuts

1 cup salted cashews

4 cups cooked jasmine rice

1. *For the sauce:* In a bowl, whisk together the chicken stock, soy sauce, vinegar, hoisin, honey, Sriracha, sesame oil, ginger, red pepper flakes, and cornstarch. Set aside.

2. *For the chicken:* In a large nonstick skillet or wok, heat the canola oil over medium-high heat.

3. Season the sliced chicken with salt and black pepper. When the oil is hot, add the chicken to the skillet in batches, browning on each side. Make sure not to overcrowd the skillet. The chicken will cook quickly, 2 to 3 minutes on each side. Transfer the chicken to a plate and repeat until all the chicken is cooked.

4. Reduce the heat to medium and add the carrots and snow peas, sautéing until they are soft, but left with a slight bite, about 3 minutes. Add the garlic and water chestnuts and cook for 1 minute.

5. Reduce the heat to low and return the cooked chicken to the pan. Add the reserved sauce and the cashews, stir together to combine, and cook until the sauce thickens, about 1 minute.

6. Serve hot over jasmine rice.

Margarita-Marinated Skirt Steak with Pineapple-Avocado Salsa

❧ *Serves 4* ❧

I knew I wanted to include at least one boozy recipe in my book. I'm not a huge fan of spirits in my baking, but adding a little happy juice to my cooking is something I do quite often! The first time I tried this recipe I added way too much tequila. Turns out while a strong margarita is nice, a strong tequila marinade is not so nice. I wanted the meat to taste like the first drink at a party, not the fifth. So scaling down on the tequila a little bit and letting the meat marinate only a few hours is the sweet spot. And adding the sweet and spicy salsa on top sends this steak to the next level. Don't worry if tequila isn't your thing; you can easily leave it out.

STEAK AND MARINADE:

1½ pounds skirt steak

3 tablespoons lime juice

3 tablespoons olive oil

2 tablespoons tequila

1 tablespoon Cointreau

1 teaspoon ground coriander

1 teaspoon ground cumin

SALSA:

1 cup finely diced fresh pineapple

1 avocado, diced

¼ cup finely diced red onion

1 jalapeño, seeded and diced

1 clove garlic, minced

2 tablespoons lime juice

Salt and pepper

1. *For the steak and marinade:* Place the skirt steak in a shallow bowl or a large zip-top bag. In a bowl, mix together the lime juice, olive oil, tequila, Cointreau, coriander, and cumin. Pour the marinade over the steak, coating completely. Allow the steak to marinate for 3 hours.

2. *For the salsa:* In a medium bowl, combine the pineapple, avocado, red onion, jalapeño, and garlic. Add the lime juice and toss to coat. Season with salt and pepper to taste. Cover and refrigerate until ready to use.

3. When ready to serve, preheat a grill to high. Grill the steak 3 to 5 minutes on each side for medium doneness, depending on thickness. Allow the steak to rest for 10 minutes before slicing.

4. Serve the steak topped with salsa.

ACKNOWLEDGMENTS

*T*o those who held my hand and cheered me on along the way, I thank you times infinity. This book was very much a collaborative effort. My family, friends, and website readers all had a huge hand in what you have just (hopefully) read. The support that I receive on a daily basis is more than any one person deserves.

CHRIS: you are my love, my friend, and my one and only. Without you this would have never happened. I love you.

CHRISTOPHER, DAVID, JAKE, AND MAX, MY "CHIEF TASTE TESTERS": Thank you for always being willing to try my latest cookie, even when they "aren't your favorite." You inspire me daily. I love you all to the moon and am forever proud of each of you.

DAD AND ISA: I am so very lucky to have you as parents. Dad, you have helped make me the person I am today, and because of you I will never not know what it feels like to be special, important, and loved. Isa, you hold a dear place in my heart for always. I couldn't have finished this book on time without you. Thank you for being the best stepmom and kitchen assistant around!

KRISTAN: You're my ace. Your friendship throughout the process of writing this book, before and forever after, is my golden ticket. I love you.

I am beyond blessed to have friends who cheer me on endlessly, who are always willing to try out my latest sweet treat, and who jumped at the chance to help me test some of the recipes that made it into this book.

ANGIE, ANNE, CAROLYN, CHERYL, CHRISTINE, GRACE, GRETCHEN, KAREN, KRISTA, AND PETE: Thank you all not only for testing the recipes in this book but also for celebrating my success more than I deserve. Having a squad like you guys makes life way more fun.

SHERYL AND KEITH: I love you both, and the Neat Nacho will be in the next book for sure.

CHRISTIE: You have been my sounding board over the past few years, which I know is not an easy task. Your willingness to help at a moment's notice, try out a "bad" recipe, or just listen to all the book drama is a part-time job in and of itself. Your friendship means the world to me.

KEITH: I just want to give you a special thanks for always being willing to take a pie off my hands. Calories look better on you, my friend.

TO THE TEAM AT GALLERY/SIMON & SCHUSTER: You have been incredible over the course of the book-making process. I have felt true support from start to finish. You've made every step of this book enjoyable.

ELANA: My personal cheerleader! There isn't an author out there who wouldn't be lucky to have you as their editor. Your support and enthusiasm are unwavering. You have listened, understood, and supported every one of my ideas, steered me in the right direction when those ideas weren't on point, and done it all with a positive attitude like none other. I am so thankful for that Pumpkin Dump Cake recipe that brought us together!

ANDY: I couldn't have done this without you! You've listened, advised, and been my champion. Thank you for truly believing in my ideas.

TO MY COOKIES & CUPS FRIENDS: You are the reason that I am here on the pages of this book. I thank the universe every day that there are humans out there in the world I've never even met who rally behind me. How crazy it that? The Internet makes so many things possible, but just the fact that it brings us all together over our common love of butter and sugar makes my heart happy. I have the best job in all the world, thanks to you.

INDEX

Page numbers in *italics* refer to illustrations.